HAUNTED CAPE COD'S SEA CAPTAINS, SHIPWRECKS, AND SPIRITS

Other Pelican Titles by Barbara Sillery

The Haunting of Cape Cod and the Islands
Haunted Cape Cod
The Haunting of Louisiana
Haunted Louisiana
The Haunting of Mississippi

HAUNTED CAPE COD'S SEA CAPTAINS, SHIPWRECKS, AND SPIRITS

BARBARA SILLERY

Haunted America

PELICAN PUBLISHING
New Orleans 2022

*The word "Pelican" and the depiction of a pelican are
trademarks of Arcadia Publishing Company Inc. and are
registered in the U.S. Patent and Trademark Office.*

ISBN 9781455626823
Ebook ISBN 9781455626830

Photographs by Barbara Sillery unless otherwise indicated

Printed in the United States of America
Published by Pelican Publishing
New Orleans, LA
www.pelicanpub.com

To Glinda Schafer, an extraordinary artist and an extraordinary friend.
Thank you for all the years of being there for me.

Contents

An anonymous sea captain's wife at the Colonial House Inn in Yarmouth Port.

Prologue

There are three sorts of people; those who are alive, those who are dead, and those who are at sea.
  —Old Capstan Chantey, attributed to Anacharsis, sixth century BC

Cape Cod juts out into the Atlantic an arm with clenched fist, daring all who challenge her rugged coast ringed by treacherous shoals. Ancient mariners to and from this island haven have been explorers, conquerors, merchants . . . and pirates. On Cape Cod, these men—and women—have ventured forth to put food on the table, bring back exotic goods for trade, hunt whales, and return home to revel in this mysterious and magical place where souls of the dead linger on.

Clipper ships, packet ships, whale boats, and steamers left home ports on Cape Cod to navigate through perfect storm, after storm, after storm. There was a price to pay—ships foundered in the gales, resulting in a high death rate for crews and passengers. Given the length of the whaling voyages, averaging two to three years, sea captains were often accompanied by their wives and children. Capt. Caleb Hamblin's son Sylvanus was born at sea to his wife, Emily, in 1869 while on board the whaler *Eliza Adams*. Other infants did not make it to celebrate their first year.

The spirits of those who survived and settled back as landlubbers on their beloved Cape Cod refuse to leave. They have tales to tell, adventures to share, and a certain stubbornness that will not be dispelled. A belief in the afterlife is not required to enjoy their stories.

Lagniappe: Each of the chapters ends with *lagniappe* (lan yap), a Creole term for a little something extra. When a customer makes a purchase, the merchant often includes a small gift. The tradition dates back to the seventeenth century in France. When weighing the grain, the shop keeper would add a few extra kernels *pour la nappe* (for the cloth), as some of the grains tended to stick to the fibers of the material. In New Orleans, where I lived for more than three decades, lagniappe is an accepted daily practice. It is a form of good will, like the thirteenth rose in a bouquet of a dozen long-stemmed roses. The lagniappe at the end of each chapter offers additional background on the ghost or haunted site—perhaps just enough more to entice you to visit these Cape Cod locales and seek your own conclusions. Addresses for these haunted sites can be found at the end of this book; contacting the ghosts is up to you.

HAUNTED CAPE COD'S SEA CAPTAINS, SHIPWRECKS, AND SPIRITS

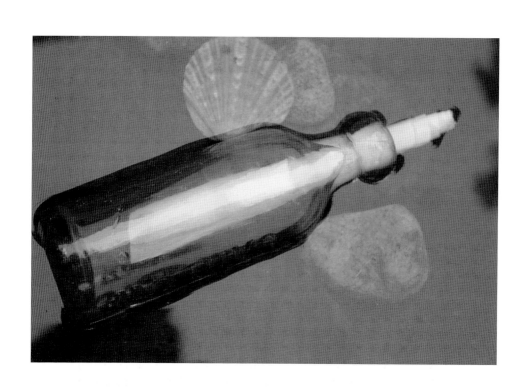

1

Message in a Bottle

On board the Pacific, *from L'pool to N. York. Ship going down . . .
confusion on board. Icebergs around us on every side. I know I cannot
escape. . . .*

—Wm. Graham

In 1861, a waterlogged "message" in a bottle found adrift near
the Hebrides, an archipelago off the west coast of Scotland,
was reputed to be the only vestige left of the *Pacific,* a luxury
oceangoing steamer. Investigation into the ship's manifest revealed
crewmember Robert Graham as the likely note writer resigned to
his fate.

On January 25, 1856, Aza Eldridge, a legendary sea captain
from Yarmouth Port on Cape Cod, set sail from Liverpool,
England to New York. Ships sailing before him reported large
icefields in the North Atlantic. The seas were brutal. When
Eldridge's ship, the *Pacific,* failed to appear at her final destination,
it was generally concluded she'd sunk after colliding with a large
mass of ice.

The *Pacific* vanished with all aboard. Forty-five passengers
and 141 crew, including Captain Eldridge, were never heard
from again—except for the one desperate scribbled message. The
mystery of the lost ship and her highly skilled captain remains
officially unresolved despite two additional tantalizing clues.

Search efforts to find the *Pacific* were launched after the ship's
overdue arrival. The Collins Line, which owned the missing ocean
liner, sent the *Alabama,* and the United States Navy sent the *Arctic;*

A large oil painting of the Pacific. (Collection of the Historical Society of Old Yarmouth)

neither found any trace. Yet, a week after the search concluded, the Scottish steamer *Edinburgh*, crossing through the same area, reported debris—oak doors with white handles and wooden windows like those designed for a ship's passenger cabin—floating about. The report offered little comfort to the shocked maritime community.

Then in 1992, nearly 136 years after the disappearance of the *Pacific*, another enigmatic clue from the deep: in the seas off of North Wales, divers discovered a wreck they believed to be the *Pacific*. The hull of the wooden ship was lying in two large sections approximately three miles apart. Some of the cargo on the seabed matched items on the *Pacific*'s manifest. Unfortunately, neither of the clues—the debris or the wreck—conclusively identified the *Pacific*.

In 1912, fifty-six years after the disappearance of the *Pacific*, another ocean liner, touted as the world's newest and most luxurious, also had a fatal encounter with an iceberg. Like the unconfirmed wreck of the *Pacific*, the hull of the *Titanic* was found in two sections about a third of a mile apart. Unlike the *Pacific*, the sinking of the *Titanic* has been well documented. Survivors' accounts were harrowing. The 1985 discovery of the wreck of the *Titanic* by a joint French-American expedition, led by Jean-Louis Michel of IFREMER and Robert Ballard of Cape Cod's Woods Hole Oceanographic Institution, left no doubt of the *Titanic*'s fate. The fate of the *Pacific*, her crew, and her captain has been

A striking portrait of Capt. Aza Eldridge. (Collection of the Historical Society of Old Yarmouth)

consigned to a message in a bottle. The question often posed at the time was: did Captain Eldridge, in a rush to set a record time for the crossing from Liverpool to New York, push his ship too hard, ignoring adverse weather conditions? If so, will the *Pacific,* now a reputed ghost ship, and her haunted captain, resurface, condemned to wandering the seas for all eternity?

In maritime lore, Capt. Aza Eldridge was a rock star. Prior to the *Pacific,* he stood at the helm of the clipper ship *Red Jacket* and set a world sailing speed record that has never been broken. In 1854, on her maiden voyage from New York to Liverpool, the *Red Jacket* arrived in thirteen days, one hour, and twenty-five minutes. To date, no commercial sailing ship has ever surpassed that time.

The Red Jacket *set a world sailing record. This painting is by nineteenth-century nautical artist Axel William Torgerson.*

Sagoyewatha, Red Jacket, on display at the Captain Bangs Hallet House Museum in Yarmouth Port.

The *Red Jacket* was said to be one of the greatest Yankee clipper ships ever to sail, and her first captain, Aza Eldridge, a true-born American sailor of unequaled daring and skill.

The 251-foot *Red Jacket* launched in November of 1853. The ship's figurehead was a life-size carving of Seneca chief Sagoyewatha, another extraordinary individual. During the American Revolution, Sagoyewatha was known as Red Jacket, for the color of the jacket given to him by the British.

Following the Revolutionary War, Sagoyewatha, said to be an eloquent orator, protested White missionary influence on Seneca customs, religion, and language. Sagoyewatha, Red Jacket, was buried with honors in Buffalo, New York.

Sadly, Red Jacket's namesake ship met an ignominious end. Sold to a Portuguese shipping company in 1883, the *Red Jacket* became a coal hauler. In 1885, she was driven ashore in a gale off the Madeira Islands. The watery grave of the *Red Jacket,* once considered the stateliest of the large American clippers, remains unmarked. But as in all good nautical lore, the ghost of her first captain, Aza Eldridge, appeared and, with a sharp snap of his hand to his forehead, gave the *Red Jacket* a farewell salute. A line from Shakespeare, "Not for her a watery end, but a new life beginning on a stranger shore," would be a fitting epitaph for this once noble ship and her lineage.

Lagniappe: Whaling was a family business. Aza Eldridge had two brothers, John and Oliver, both noted sea captains. Whaling families often intermarried. The former Anna Eldridge was the wife of Capt. Bangs Hallet and the daughter of Capt. Aza Eldridge's uncle Reuben Eldridge. Since Aza Eldridge's former home in Yarmouth Port is currently a private residence, the nearby Captain Bangs Hallet House Museum became a fitting home for the large oil painting of the *Red Jacket,* depicted off the coast of Cape Horn. The painting of the *Red Jacket,* once captained by Aza Eldridge, was a gift to the Historical Society of Old Yarmouth from the Woods Hole Oceanographic Institution.

2

Whose House Is This?

Merchant Thomas Thacher was described as a "God-fearing man" intent on "driving out the devil." In the 1840s, Thacher operated a store in old Yarmouth Port and then expanded his space with a Greek Revival addition for his personal living quarters. He sold the home in 1850 to sea captain Allen Hinckley Knowles. In 1863, Captain Knowles and fellow sea captain Bangs Hallet swapped houses, with each man believing he got the better end of the deal. However, the real winners in this house swap are the ghosts, for the spirits here have the final say.

Second owner Allen Hinckley Knowles, a renowned clipper-

The Captain Bangs Hallet House Museum, with its ghostly inhabitants.

Portrait of Anna Hallet in the parlor.

ship captain, swapped houses with Captain Hallet when the latter and his wife, Anna, were looking to downsize from the larger home they owned on Old King's Highway.

The grief-stricken parents had lost all but two of their eight children to various tragedies and needed an escape from the overwhelming memories.

In death, a few former residents appear to have joined the ranks of the paranormal. Anna Hallet lived in the home for over thirty years. As the wife of a ship's captain, Anna's spirit clings to her thrifty ways. She runs the proverbial tight ship, shutting doors, closing windows, and turning off lights. Following a recent tour of the house, a visitor asked the tour guide if the home was haunted. The startled guide hesitated a few beats before replying, "We have a lamp in the parlor that keeps shutting itself off. We turn it on and, as soon as we leave the room, it goes off. We took it to an electrician to check it out, and he said there is nothing wrong with it; it stayed on for him." The tour guide furtively glanced back at the parlor, as if afraid someone would overhear. "I think it's Anna Hallet, her ghost. She was very frugal. She doesn't like the light being left on if no one is in the room."

The ghost of original owner Thomas Thacher has his own issues. He is blamed for the heavy foot pounding up and down the stairs. Some believe that Thomas has seller's remorse; his spirit roams the house in vain, seeking the store he owned.

After his death, the store was severed from the existing kitchen and moved from the site. Those who have seen Thomas say he wears his clothes inside out as he wakes frantic each morning trying to solve the riddle of the missing store.

Even the 120-plus-year-old beech tree on the fifty-acre grounds has garnered a haunted reputation. Carvings of weeping beeches on tombstones were prevalent in early-nineteenth-century New England. The drooping branches symbolize the "weeping" or mourning for a loved one. It was a common practice to place branches of the beech in the coffins of the deceased and then plant young saplings over their graves with the belief that the spirit of the

Carving of a weeping beech tree on a headstone in a Cape Cod cemetery.

dead would rise up through the trees. Grieving parents Anna and Bangs Hallet had to process the loss of six children.

Visitors to the Hallet weeping beech are drawn to its intertwined branches that create soothing pockets for rest and reflection. On occasion, their quiet retreat has been interrupted by the spectral sight of the silhouette of an older man, his shoulders stooped in grief, lingering briefly nearby. Could this be the stoic Captain Hallet hiding his sorrow from his beloved Anna over the loss of children who died too young?

The haunted beech tree where Capt. Bangs Hallet has been seen grieving for his children.

A portrait of Capt. Bangs Hallet shares the parlor with one of his beloved wife.

The Historical Society of Old Yarmouth manages the Captain Bangs Hallet House, listed on the National Register of Historic Places, as a museum open for tours. The Society acknowledges it must deal with tales of personal tragedy, ongoing preservation challenges, and the often clashing personalities of a retinue of ghosts.

Lagniappe: A real-life mystery added to the turmoil surrounding the house museum. One summer night in 1988, two men forced their way inside, tied up the female caretaker, and made off with six nineteenth-century paintings, including portraits of Captain Bangs and his daughter, along with a miniature painting of his wife, Anna. The bold robbers also stole 200 pieces of scrimshaw and a thirteenth-century Chinese artifact. The total value of the stolen items was over one hundred thousand dollars. According to newspaper reports, the thieves wore gloves, carried a police scanner, and appeared to be working from a list of specific items. The robbers were never caught, nor were the paintings and scrimshaw ever recovered.

Based on photographs of the original paintings, Yarmouth artist Heather Braginton-Smith recreated images of the stolen portraits. Her renderings hang in silent rebuke to the thieves who robbed a town of a chapter of its history.

The Sandwich Glass Museum is home to phantoms William and Rebecca.

3

Phantom Couple on Call

Hannah Rebecca Crowell and William Howes Burgess await the pleasure of your company at the Sandwich Glass Museum. Seek them out, and this phantom couple will share their sad saga.

A faint blush brushed her high cheekbones the first time fifteen-year-old Rebecca (as she preferred to be called) met William Burgess. The dashing, dark-haired sailor stood in the parlor of the home of her wealthy great-uncle Benjamin Burgess. Rebecca, a quiet country girl, had traveled with her parents, Paul and Lydia Crowell, from their West Sandwich home to Boston. Rebecca lowered her thick lashes and tried not to stare when she was introduced to her twenty-year-old distant cousin William, a native of Brewster and already a successful mariner.

William felt equally drawn to the attractive young woman with her shy demeanor. A four-year courtship began as William's sea voyages took him around the globe. Fueled by letters expressing devotion and promises, the couple's mutual admiration grew. In his letters, William wrote of his lofty ideals, his habit of daily prayer, and promised he would never swear in her presence. Rebecca was suitably impressed. Returning from his last port of call, William proposed marriage, and Rebecca accepted. She prepared her hope chest. On August 5, 1852, eighteen-year-old Hannah Rebecca Crowell married twenty-three-year-old William Howes Burgess at the West Sandwich Methodist church. Their rings were engraved with the words "I will never marry again." Dorothy Hogan-Schofield, the curator of the Sandwich Glass Museum, observed that "many people think that Rebecca

Hannah Rebecca Crowell Burgess as a young bride.

did this, but it was in fact William." Both William and Rebecca fulfilled the promise etched in their golden wedding bands—just not the way either had intended.

The couple's ghostly forms appear (as holograms) in the recreated dining room of the Sandwich Glass Museum. The widow Burgess materializes and whispers in a weary voice, "My beloved husband William, God rest his soul. I have missed him for thirty-four years. He was twenty-seven and a captain when he died. I was only his wife for four short years."

Fortunately, Rebecca kept a journal, so the record of what unfolded in the time leading up to William's death has been preserved. Three months after their honeymoon, newlywed

Rebecca, wistful and sad, at her dining room table.

William left for sea as the captain of the *Whirlwind*. After a miserable solo journey without his bride, William decided that Rebecca would be with him on all future voyages. On February 4, 1854, the clipper ship *Whirlwind* set sail from New York to San Francisco with husband William at the helm, and wife Rebecca working on her sea legs. "O how the waves did come over the side of the ship . . . the ship was pitching and rolling and I was not able to walk for fear of falling down. Then I was seasick too . . . it was two weeks before I could even sit up at all. I could scarcely keep my equilibrium."

One night, after she recuperated from her ordeal, William called Rebecca up on deck, and she became enamored with the sea: "I never witnessed such a beautiful sight in my life as tonight at sunset . . . all the colors of the rainbow arranged in fantastic order."

Rebecca was eager to absorb it all, and William took great pleasure in teaching her. "During our first voyage, it took 131 days to travel from Boston to San Francisco . . . yet Rebecca took delight in every aspect of that voyage. Not every woman would set sail with their husband."

For her part, Rebecca had only one issue with the husband she idolized: "I am so happy in love with my husband, yet one thing grieves me; he does not carry out those principles he once professed to sustain." The habit this unreformed sea captain could never overcome? William swore.

Within the first two years of her marriage, Rebecca crossed the equator eleven times and learned to navigate a ship. The experience and acquired skills saved her life and that of thirty crew members on an 1856 voyage around the world on the clipper ship *Challenger,* when William became sick and there was no one to direct the ship.

William had dysentery. With the help of the first mate, Henry Windsor, Rebecca supervised the loading of guano at the Chincha Islands. The crew of the *Challenger* grew increasingly alarmed over the weakened condition of their captain, and Windsor refused to accept responsibility for the ship. Although Rebecca had never captained a vessel, she ordered the anchors up and set sail for Valparaiso, Chile, their next intended port.

For twenty days, Rebecca commanded the ship, taking time only to go below deck to comfort her husband. Tragically, Rebecca was able to hold on to husband's body but not his soul. The specter of William's widow fidgets in the dining room chair. She hesitates before disclosing her beloved's final moments. "We were so happy together, and then my dear husband became gravely ill off the coast of Chile. I loved him so dearly and worked so hard to nurse him back to health."

William died in her arms on December 11, 1856. They were in the Pacific Ocean off the coast of South America. Burial at sea was the customary way to dispose of a body, as it was considered bad luck to have a corpse on board. Rebecca could not bear the thought of tossing William into the fathomless sea, so she held her ground against the superstitious crew and sailed the *Challenger* into Valparaiso with William's body on board.

Rebecca Burgess booked passage on the *Harriet Irving* for herself and her husband's remains. Capt. William Howes Burgess was interred in the Sagamore Cemetery in Sandwich. For the obelisk that serves as his headstone, Rebecca composed a poem. The last verse reads:

> Oh! I have loved too fondly
> And a gracious Father's hand
> Hath removed my cherished idol
> To a brighter better land.
> But this last hope is left me
> To cheer my stricken heart,
> In that blest world to meet thee
> And never, never part.
> Rebecca

More than fifty men offered proposals of marriage to the attractive widow. She spurned them all. William's wedding band, with its engraved vow, remained on her finger until her death at age eighty-two.

William and Rebecca's ghostly images do not appear simultaneously at the Sandwich Glass Museum. Instead, as if in some disconnected dance, they take turns sitting at the head of the table. Unlike his wife, Capt. William Burgess has not aged. His figure takes shape as a robust young man in his late twenties. Dead since 1856, his thoughts rest with his spouse. "My dear wife, Rebecca, she held to our solemn vow never to marry again. Who would have thought I would get so horribly sick at only twenty-

William, longing to be reunited with Rebecca.

seven? There we were, just married, and I the captain of the *Challenger*. We saw places together that most people would only dream about . . . I was so proud of my ship and so in love with Rebecca. We had great plans, she and I."

The transparent apparition in a dark blue captain's jacket is amazed by his wife's grit and courage. "Did you know that as I lay in my sick bed, she managed to navigate the ship back to port. . . . Yes, Rebecca, a woman, what a lady! I knew she was special when I first met her."

As the captain's image starts to fade, his voice catches. His parting words are for Rebecca. "How I wish a place at that table was set for me. How I wish I could come back, take her in my arms, and never let her go. I loved her so very much. May we meet in heaven!"

After burying William, twenty-two-year-old Rebecca continued writing in her journal about her exploits during their brief marriage. Author Megan Taylor Shockley, who wrote about Rebecca, explains that "a lot of Victorian women . . . used their journals to make sense of their lives. What's really important about Rebecca Burgess is that she was able to create an image of herself that people liked, embraced, and wanted to discuss after her death."

Although she "retired from active life," Rebecca enjoyed having close friends and family for dinner and "engaging my guests in conversation."

When making a visit to a reputed haunted site, it is often disappointing when the cadre of ghosts within refuses to make their presence known. At the Sandwich Glass Museum, Rebecca and William are immortalized as holograms, creations of the digital age—a phantom couple eager to make your acquaintance.

Lagniappe: Finding Rebecca and William can be a bit tricky. Navigating the warren of fifteen exhibit rooms in the Sandwich Museum requires perseverance. More than six thousand glass objects in brilliant hues of ruby red, royal amethyst, canary yellow, cobalt blue, pearl pink, opalescent white, and emerald green are

An amazing array of colors and shapes in the museum.

mesmerizing. Distractions are at every turn, each goblet a regal chalice to observe, each Lacy plate, a coronet for the gods. Some visitors go full circle, exit through the gift shop, and never meet the delightful couple. To avoid the same mistake, use the guided map, and steer the circuitous route. Bypass the glassblowing demonstration, the Introduction to the Story of Glass, the Mixing Room, and the Hirschmann Theatre. Enter and exit the *Art of the Glass Blower* exhibit, and then make a sharp right from the Mold-Blown and Early Press Glass Rooms into the Lacy Glass area. From there, look to the left for the entrance to Mid-Nineteenth Century Pressed Glass. Keep going straight through Pattern

Glass, and make a hard right. Look overhead for the sign that reads "The Hannah Rebecca Burgess Dining Room." If you find yourself in Post-Civil War Production or Threaded and Decorated Glass, you have gone too far. The entrance will be dark, but feel for the top blue button, and press it. Have a seat on the bench, be patient, and in a few moments, you will hear a woman gasp: "Oh, you are not my dinner guests!" Ever the gracious hostess, Rebecca's hologram comes into focus as she announces, "Let me light the lamps and candles so we can see each other." And so her story begins.

Susan's ghost lives at the Simmons Homestead.

4

Don't Let Susan Out

Bill Putman acts like an over-protective father when it comes to the little ghost girl who haunts the Simmons Homestead Inn in Hyannis Port. Putman worries that if she ran off, she wouldn't know what to do, and something might happen to her. It happened once before. "The first time Susan got out was in 1833, and she drowned in the pond. She was the daughter of Lemuel Simmons."

Sea captain Lemuel Baker Simmons and his family lived in the farmhouse that was built by his father, Sylvanus Simmons, around 1810. Lemuel and his wife, Temperance, had nine children, four girls and five boys. Temperance died in September of 1841. Five months later, in February 1842, Lemuel married a widow, Eliza Bearse, and they had two children, a girl and a boy. According to the 1850 Federal Census, all of these children were alive and living at the farmhouse, but little Susan is not listed. The twenty-acre pond where the seven-year-old child drowned stills exits and is now owned by the town.

Bill Putman and his wife, Suzy, had always intended to own and operate a country inn. "We felt it was a good way to retire." Sadly, Putman's wife died before their plan became a reality. "I didn't want to go back to the corporate world," says soft-spoken Putman, "and then this came on the market. I bought it in 1988 and have had it [ever since]. I did not believe in ghosts and had never seen a ghost until I came here." At the time of his purchase, the house had been a summer home for the Groves family. "It had no heat or anything like that." When Putman began his massive, one-man restoration, he discovered he had a little spirit to keep him company.

"When I first came here, I was painting walls and stuff like that. I was upstairs in the back hallway, and I sort of begin to see something out of the corner of my eye. I hear a giggle, and I see her duck around the corner. I have never experienced anything like that. She had long brown hair, wore a white dress, and was about four feet tall. I guess she was checking to see that I wasn't screwing up her daddy's house."

Initially, Putman did not have a name for his blithe spirit. A psychic who was staying in room number five, the Owl Room, came down to breakfast one morning and asked the innkeeper if he knew he had a ghost. Putman replied, "Yes, I do, but how did

The Owl Room may have been Susan's bedroom.

you know?" The woman informed him that "I was up all night talking to her, and she told me her name is Susan." After staying in the same room, other guests, unaware of little Susan's tragic death, have also sat down to breakfast and talked about having a strange sensation that they were sharing the room with "a presence." They described the presence as "friendly and happy."

Putman describes Susan as a shy but curious ghost. When a female guest leaves the room, Susan will inspect her make-up. She'll uncap lipsticks, dip brushes in eye shadow, and open compacts. She does not tidy up after herself very well. Putman believes she does this on purpose, so that people will notice that she's around. "She likes attention, and she deserves all she can get."

Susan's "foster father" and protector worries about her. "As more and more people heard about our ghost, the ghost hunters started coming around, so I am careful who I let in because she deserves better than that. One ghost hunting couple tried to take photographs, and the next morning, they got up and the film had been rerolled— there was nothing on it." Putman smiles. "She got them."

The Simmons Homestead has ten guestrooms in the main house and an additional two in the attic, which have been used by staff. In the winter of 1991, Felicia Shea worked as the assistant innkeeper. She remembered going to her attic bedroom and finding the "drawers of my dresser were pulled open." Shea also noticed that a few of her personal items were out of place on her dressing table. Since no was else was staying in the main house at the time, Shea attributed the childish pranks to a small spirit who wanted to explore. To entertain her inquisitive ghost, the assistant innkeeper picked up a book from the nightstand and began to read out loud. "She read *Forever Amber* to her and started calling our ghost Amber," says Putman, who prefers Susan as a more appropriate choice of name. Shea continued her habit of reading to "Amber" whenever she felt her presence but switched to a more suitable selection of reading material—children's books borrowed from the local library. "I think Susan kept hanging out with Felicia because she thought of her as a big sister," considers Putman.

Putman believes that prior to her death, Susan would have played in the attic as a child, running back and forth with her sisters and brothers. He has also noticed over the years that Susan's tiny spirit seems to prefer female guests as her new playmates, with one exception, Putman's stepson, Craig. "He experienced a presence in the upstairs hallway near room five when he was thirteen years old." Since room five is Susan's favorite in the afterlife, the assumption is that it might have been hers as a child.

Indeed, the current animal kingdom décor of the entire inn has built-in kid appeal. "It started with my wife; she did needlepoint wall hangings of birds. When I came down here, I didn't plan on making all the rooms have animal themes; it just sort of grew. The Elephant Room was the first, and well . . . damn thing now is completely out of control."

Guests have their choice of the Cat Suite, Dogs Room (there is a bulletin board where people can pin up pictures of their dogs), Rabbit Hutch Room, Geese with a Few Cows Room, Jungle Room, Fish Aquarium Room, or Birds, Butterflies, and Parrots Room. Susan's preferred haunt, room five, is the Owl Room. The adjacent annex houses the Cape Cod Critters and Little Critters Rooms and the Horse and Hound Suite.

The amiable host of the Simmons Homestead, a Yale graduate with a degree in geology and MBA in marketing from New York University, is now a self-professed animal addict. "I started putting some critters around as decorations." These decorations peer from shelves, preen on paintings, posture in needlepoint wall hangings, and perch on bars suspended from the ceilings. "I can't abide empty spaces," confesses the innkeeper.

Putman has made an attempt to tame the animal overload with a link to the home's history. "Last winter, I kind of toned it down a little. I converted the Giraffe Room into the Dog Room, and the Elephant Room is the Atlantic Room because Lemuel Simmons was the youngest sea captain to sail the seven seas." But Putman couldn't help sneaking in a few animals when he redid the Zebra Room. "It's now the Simmons Pond Room, so it has toads and little turtles."

The Fish Aquarium Room, one of the themed bedrooms at the inn.

Animals adorn every surface of the common room.

With so many carved, enameled, appliquéd, sculpted, and stuffed animals, it's not surprising that Putman is also a caretaker of the real thing. At one time, he had thirty-three cats. Their names all start with the letter A because "I want them all to feel like alpha cats." The leaders of this feline menagerie are Abigail and her successors, Abigail One and Abigail Too.

Astair (named after Fred) is the official greeter—he welcomes every guest on arrival, follows them around the grounds, and is the last furry face they see on departure. In deference to guests who have allergies, all of the cats are banned from the main house. However, Abigail tends to ignore the rules. While guests are encouraged to explore and enjoy the Simmons Homestead

Astair (named after Fred), the official greeter.

and all of the sights of nearby Hyannis, the laid-back innkeeper does have one very important rule. A sign on the front door warns: "DON'T LET ABIGAIL IN, OR SUSAN OUT."

Abigail is one very smart, persistent cat, who does her best to have guests break Putnam's rule. As for the second half of his commandment, a seven-year-old ghost child shouldn't be tempted to roam alone outside. As Putman is fond of saying, "We welcome and enjoy little Susan. After all, this has been her house a lot longer than it's been ours."

Lagniappe: Mixed in among the merry mishmash of animal artifacts at the Simmons Homestead on Scudder Avenue in Hyannis Port are antique beds, private baths with claw-foot tubs, lace curtains, Queen Anne chairs, and cozy fireplaces. "I wanted to create a space that feels like home," says the innkeeper, who refers to himself as "the purveyor of timely tiny tidbits of trivia." The relaxed atmosphere of the inn consistently earns rave reviews. During the 1991 Robert Kennedy Memorial golf tournament, the Kennedy family rented the entire inn for a slew of high-profile guests: Dinah Shore, Carly Simon, James Woods, and former Olympic gold medal decathlon winner Bruce Jenner.

The adjacent annex serves as an adult playhouse with billiards and a barroom, where Putman houses his single malt Scotch whisky collection, featuring well more than six hundred varieties from every distillery and region in Scotland. "The main reason, other than compulsion, is that I like single malts . . . I haven't had a cold in more than thirty years—seems like as good a reason as any to hoard them and drink them." The jovial host is more than willing to have tastings with his guests and would be happy to have the ghost of Lemuel Simmons belly up to the bar, but he knows that's never going to happen. Simmons was an avowed teetotaler, and the captain sailed out of Boston Harbor on the first ship to *not* offer rum rations to its crew. That's okay with the present owner, who finds loving companionship with his feline menagerie that hangs out here on every available space.

Putman's single malt whisky collection.

Toad Hall houses antique cars.

Putman, a former race car driver, also collects sports cars and owns fifty-eight of them, all red. He owns vintage English Triumphs, Austin Healeys, Jaguars, and MGs. Most of them are stored in Toad Hall, a series of sheds between the main house and the annex. Putman explains his choice of the name for the antique car garage. "It's from *The Wind in the Willows.* Toad was the main character, and he was fascinated with the new motor cars of the late 1800s." Bill Putman loves them all: cars, cats, Scotch whisky, and Susan.

The haunted Colonial House Inn, where ghosts run rampant.

5

Must Love Ghosts

A disgruntled guest of the Colonial House Inn in Yarmouth Port complained that no one told her the inn was haunted. She insisted that a warning sign be posted out front: "MUST LOVE GHOSTS."

"We lasted only two nights due to the ghosts who bothered us . . . My husband saw this lady in white when we first arrived. . . . At three-thirty a.m. we were awakened by a blood-curdling scream. The next night, I left the light on all night and did not sleep one wink. . . . I would never stay here again or recommend this inn to anyone unless they loved ghosts."

Owner Malcom Perna is unfazed. A translucent lady who tends to an invisible garden, a rocking chair that turns of its own volition to face a wall, a non-existent baby crying through the night—he simply adds the paranormal observations to his growing "Ghost Ledger." "I knew nothing about ghost stories associated with the property when I purchased it, and I couldn't have cared less." Now, keeping track of the ghostly apparitions and their favorite hot spots has become an entertaining sidebar to his duties as innkeeper.

"People started telling me about the ghosts here, so I started recording it. I would write the date, sometimes people's names, sometimes not, but what was more important was what was said and what area of the inn they were in when they saw or heard or did whatever this was. And [since 1979] I have been amazed; if the same type of story has happened or been reported to me in the same area—and it's a big property—it gives credence. To just hear that you got a voice somewhere in the inn doesn't mean a thing, but if I can connect it to a room or area where I have had a report before, then there is a credibility level. But if I can't, that's okay too."

Paranormal activities at the inn run the gamut. The apparitions—male or female, adults, teens, or babies—are all connected to previous occupants from several centuries of ownership. A portrait of a fearsome sea captain with a thick white beard hangs above the fireplace in the Oak Room, one of three dining areas on the first floor of the inn. Perna acknowledges the portrait with a quick nod. "This is Capt. Fay Parker, the last of about eleven sea captains who owned this house. This portrait was done in 1900." Adhering to his policy of letting each visitor encounter and/or identify a specific ghost based on their personal experience, Perna will not reveal if Captain Fay haunts the Oak Room. Instead, the innkeeper gives an overview of the history of the house, and, in the process, introduces a few of the likely contenders who have lived here and never left.

"Essentially, the house was built in the 1730s as a Federal-style two-story building with a hip roof. Originally built by the Josiah Ryder family, it was acquired by the Capt. Joseph Eldridge family, and they had sea captain after sea captain after sea captain." For the next one-hundred-plus years, the home was known as the Eldridge House. A Doric-columned portico altered the style of the front façade from Federal to Victorian. "They were making things grander. . . . You see, these sea captains weren't just sea captains . . . they were shipping magnets. By the time the 1850s came . . . these same two families, the Eldridges and the Thachers [relatives by marriage], had moved the center of operations to Boston, so this would have been their summer home."

Sadly, this grand summer home was the site of numerous deaths. Capt. Joseph Eldridge lived here as early as 1804. He and his wife had nine children; four died before reaching their first birthday. In his will, the captain left the house to his youngest child, Azariah. Dr. Azariah Eldridge and his wife, Ellen, had only one child, who died at a young age. Both Azariah and Ellen suffered from poor health. When Azariah died in 1856, Ellen was

Capt. Fay Parker stares down from his portrait in the Oak Room.

too ill to attend the funeral. Having no heir, Ellen left the house to the First Congregational Church.

"Three hundred and fifty years . . . that is not unusual, childbirths and deaths," says Perna. What veers into the realm of the exceptional are the wails of sick babies echoing in one room of the inn. "That thing is consistent, and it is always the same part of the house. You hear a baby crying and there is no baby."

Another peculiar manifestation could be linked to the same poor babies and their worried mothers. In a bedroom in the main house a rocking chair has been found to turn itself around during the night and face the wall. "This is a reoccurring event," confirms the owner. Although the ability of an inanimate object to move at will defies logic, Perna knows it is also a case of the rocking chair being in the wrong position. "To be perfectly honest, I am familiar with the alterations made to the house. That blank wall the rocking chair turns to face used to have a window." The real debate seems to be whether the rocking chair possesses a supernatural ability or whether a mother's loving spirit turns the chair back to its original position so she can lull her colicky baby to sleep.

The Colonial House Inn has eleven guest rooms in the manor house and ten in the converted Carriage House. The Carriage House also has a two-story cupola. "Originally it was a small, single one, and then they built a top story to house a water tank. They used a windmill to pump the water up there, and gravity feeds the water throughout the complex." Perna boasts that the Eldridges had "indoor plumbing before there was such a thing: this is called having money." These sea captains also employed stable boys to care for their horses and carriage. One forlorn lad took his own life.

"I do know that a young, sixteen-year-old boy committed suicide here inside the carriage house. He hung himself." The innkeeper conducted an extensive background check. "I have studied the archives of the *Register* newspaper about the events that have occurred. I am past president of the historical society, so obviously a real history of this house, not a paranormal history of the house, is very important to me." Nevertheless, Perna meticulously records each and every account claiming to hear the voice of a young boy crying in the carriage house along with reported sounds of horses neighing. With the exception of native wildlife, only well-behaved pets (limited to dogs and cats) are permitted at the inn.

Elizabeth Embler, whose parents rented out rooms during the summer season, remembers an encounter with another ghostly presence. In the slow winter season, she had her pick of bedrooms. However, room number eight proved to be a poor choice. She

A young boy hung himself in the carriage house.

awoke at night to find a stranger moving about her room. At first she was not afraid, thinking it might be a guest who had mistaken her room for theirs (it had happened before). But that time, it was different. Embler instinctively knew the figure was "not a real person." In her account to the Yarmouth Historical Society, Embler relates that the male presence was facing away with his arms folded. She watched apprehensively as he looked at one window and then turned to look out another. He was dressed in clothes of "a different generation." The phantom lingered for ten minutes and then vanished. Embler was unable to positively identify him as one of the many sea captains who lived in the house because "he was more like a shadow."

The "translucent lady in white" is another reoccurring apparition, only she haunts the grounds, not the house itself. "A lady dressed in period clothes is working in what appears to be a garden." Perna speaks in riddles. "Somewhere in the middle of an open space, she's out there in a garden that is not really a garden, but may have been a garden, not one of the gardens you see now."

The innkeeper's arms are folded across his chest. He is in the tavern, a warm inviting space just off the lobby. A black-and-white sketch of the mansion as it appeared during the 1880s looms over his shoulder. "I don't know who she was, but I know there was a garden here almost two hundred years ago, and I happen to know where." Perna turns to face the framed image of the house with its extensive front lawn, young trees, and pathways. What seems to be a glass greenhouse (no longer in existence) is to the right. Perna taps the image gently with his finger. "So, when you talk about seeing a ghost gardening in an open space, that's how I can tell whether there is validity to your story or not. Remember, I am a historian."

Many of the haunted tales associated with the inn are well known. The innkeeper has developed his own methods for ensuring that the reports from his guests are not merely a repeat of haunted tales already in circulation: he runs his version of a double-blind study.

He refuses to divulge the specific rooms where alleged hauntings

Malcom Perna will neither confirm nor deny which rooms are haunted.

have occurred. "I never say room numbers, and all the numbers [of the haunted rooms] you hear about have probably been changed. If you go online you are going to read something about room 224. There is no room number 224, but I do this intentionally." Perna doesn't want to sway or influence a guest's perception of what might happen. "I don't want to say to you, 'You are staying in room 7, and what has been reported in room 7 is that after midnight the closet door just keeps opening and closing.' And then you'll be thinking about that, and the next morning you are going to come down and say, 'Guess what, Mac? That damn door kept me awake all night!'" For Perna, when this happens, "There is no validity to what you are telling me." On the other hand, explains the innkeeper, "If you come down and say, 'You know, I was in room 7 last night—or 107 or 207—and the damn door kept opening or closing,' and there was no wind that night, I record it and look back and I see that four years before that someone else shared the same story." The innkeeper sees the needle on the plausibility factor rise a few degrees.

To deter other guests from assuming that just because there is a rocking chair in the room it is *the* rocking chair, Perna flooded the inn with them. "I have since put eight rocking chairs in various rooms and turned them all around to face the windows. Otherwise, it's out there on the internet so everyone is talking about it, and if you stay in a room with a rocking chair, you'll be convinced you saw something that didn't happen." Only Perna knows which one is the real "haunted rocking chair."

The supernatural buzz surrounding the Colonial House Inn naturally attracted the ghost hunters. "We have been investigated by paranormal groups over twenty times." With a sly smile Pena adds, "No one ever leaves those investigations empty handed."

In 2006, the Spirit Encounters Research Team (SERT), arrived ready to go to work. Prior to their arrival, Perna took down all pictures and documents that might offer clues. At the conclusion of their investigation, medium Richard Boisvere made his report to Perna. "At no time did I or any member of my team feel threatened in any way. All experiences were playful, mischievous and/or friendly. Team members experienced sensations of being touched near the dance floor . . . EVPs [Electronic Voice Phenomenon] near the Widow's Watch recorded children's voices, and the sound of footsteps running up and down stairs. A recording made at 1:45 a.m. had a child's voice whispering 'Hello.'"

CAPS, the Cape and Island Paranormal Society, also published findings on their Web site of the Colonial House Inn, which included sightings of apparitions, sounds, and moving objects. Perna says he did not make them privy to any specifics. "I just let them do their thing. I told them, 'If you guys want to find something, go find it.'" The innkeeper notes that what these groups have reported during their investigations have "matched what I have in my ledger many times. Almost always they come up with at least one match without my helping them."

As part of his blind study, Perna has flooded the house with rocking chairs.

Each year at Halloween, Perna hosts "Ghost Hunting 101" and invites a different paranormal group for the weekend affair. "It starts off with a cocktail party in the afternoon in which a paranormal group shows you the equipment, teaches you how to use it . . . and sets up the equipment to run overnight. On Saturday evening . . . you review what the equipment might have captured. Guests love it. It's the best entertainment in the world."

Malcom Perna is quite clear when it comes to his personal beliefs. "I don't feel it's my duty to prove one way or another that the inn is haunted." He pauses to let the impact of his statement settle in before continuing. "My favorite thing to say is that I have never seen a ghost! And if I ever did, he or she (the ghost) would have two choices: pay for the room for the night or do some work. Maybe that's why I have never seen a ghost."

Lagniappe: When Malcom Perna purchased the property in 1979, "It was deserted, deteriorated." However, it did meet some of his other criteria. "It had to be a *significant* home. I wanted a property that I could develop into an inn, and it had to have lawns and gardens." Along with restoring and enlarging the main house, Perna created tranquil garden spaces. The innkeeper waves his arm in the direction of the triangular-shaped Yarmouth Port Village Green. "At one time, the Eldridges and the Thachers owned all the property around here, but what people did when a son or daughter was getting married, is they said, 'Okay, we'll take a plot of this land and we'll build a house for you next door.'"

The Edward Gorey House is a prime example. "When one of the Thachers who owned this house gave parcels of his property to his two daughters, it wound up that the back of the second daughter's barn was actually on her father's property, but it didn't matter because it was all in the family." "Technically," says a complacent Perna, "the [Edward Gorey House] barn is on my property by about four or five inches. Who cares? It's done now."

Edward Gorey, the Tony award-winning set designer for the Broadway hit *Dracula,* was a good neighbor, who lived around the

Edward Gorey's home of the last years of his life.

corner from the Colonial House Inn for the last fourteen years of his life. In a March 2011, *New York Times* "News Bulletin from the Spirit World" reporter Mark Dery wrote, "The specter of Edward Gorey . . . is haunting our collective unconscious . . . His poisonously funny little picture books, deadpan accounts of murder, disaster and discreet depravity . . . established him as the master of high-camp macabre." A tour of the Edward Gorey House is the perfect paranormal follow-up to the specters at the Colonial House Inn.

Skulls and skeletons, doorknobs and rocks, bats, ravens, and

A window display at the Edward Gorey House.

a tiny Amy doll caught mid-fall on the stairs are all part of the helter-skelter ambiance of Edward Gorey's world, in which "more is happening out there than we are aware of."

Back at the Colonial House Inn, ghosts and guests are still welcome, but there's a new look to this spirited site. Following the death of owner Malcom Perna on September 15, 2015, the inn, after an extensive renovation, reopened its doors as the Chapter House, a twenty-one-room boutique hotel. The new management pays tongue-in-cheek homage to its ghosts: "When we say 'Lodging and Spirits' since 1716, we aren't kidding."

Capt. Ebenezer Harding Linnell.

6

Love Possessed

There are ghosts and there is love,
And both are present here.
To those who listen, this tale will tell
The truth of love and if it's near.
——Nicholas Sparks, *A Bend in the Road*

"Love like ours can never die!" Impaled by a spoke from his own ship's wheel, Capt. Ebenezer Linnell might have shouted this lover's litany to his beloved in his final fatal moments. His adoring wife, Rebecca, kept him close to her heart, never faltering in her devotion. Her ghostly form waits for him at the Captain Linnell House in East Orleans.

Ebenezer Harding Linnell, born in 1811 on Barley Neck Road, Orleans, married the beautiful, golden-haired Rebecca Crosby in 1835. She was twenty-one, and he was twenty-four, a young sea captain embarking on a promising career. The couple moved into a Cape Codder on the site of the present day Captain Linnell House. For the next two decades, Eben would sail around the globe on the clipper ships *Flying Mist* and *Eagle Wing*. At first, petite, four-foot-eleven-inch Rebecca accompanied her husband, but as their children grew—Helen, Florentina, Ebenezer, and Abigail—Rebecca was content to remain at home. Eben and Rebecca's love letters, preserved in Boston's Peabody Museum, are a testament to the couple's enduring devotion. Eben sought only the best for the love of his life.

Rebecca Crosby Linnell.

On a trip to France in 1850, he stayed at a shipping agent's villa in the port city of Marseilles. Captain Linnell brought the house plans back to the Cape and had his father-in-law oversee the construction of a neo-classical French villa. "They built around the Cape Codder. It's still here." Shelly Conway along with her husband, Bill, own the Captain Linnell House, now an award-winning restaurant. "Actually," says a thoughtful Shelly, "Captain Linnell was considered a show-off. Everyone in town thought he was too grand for his britches. He filled the house with furniture and fittings from Europe and the Orient." A cupola on the roof of the villa allowed Rebecca to look out over their thirty-

The Captain Linnell House, now an award-winning restaurant.

five acres of land and beyond to the shores of Cape Cod Bay near the present Skaket Beach. "Rebecca would sit up there, and when her husband's ship would come in, she would be able to see because at that time there were no trees around here. There was a 360-degree view."

In 1864, in one of the ceaseless ironies of the sea, Captain Linnell announced to his family that he was embarking on his last voyage. Off the coast of Brazil, a tropical storm tossed the ship about like a toy. The boom holding the spanker sail broke loose and smashed the captain against his wheel, where a spoke punctured one his lungs. Ebeneezer Linnell was critically injured and lived only a few days. The fifty-three-year-old master mariner was buried at sea. According to an article published in the December 1995 edition of the *Linnell Family Newsletter,* Rebecca retreated to the cupola to "read and reread the letter from the *Eagle Wing*'s first mate." The letter described Captain Linnell's "horrible and untimely death."

Restaurateur Shelly Conway describes how "after he died, Rebecca would go up to the cupola every single day for the rest of her life." Rebecca Cosby Linnell died at the age of eighty-one. The *Linnell Family Newsletter* also reports that Rebecca's lonely spirit still visits the widow's walk "wistfully looking out to sea." She searches the horizon for her captain, who will never return. Wishful visitors, however, have a problem—the entrance to Rebecca's observation post is blocked. "There is a wonderful inside staircase that leads to the cupola," explains Conway, "but the last private owners, the Hamiltons, actually put a chimney up through there." Viewed from the outside, the chimney stack is clearly visible poking through the cupola's roof. The physical obstruction has had little impact on Rebecca's spirit, as people have claimed to see Rebecca seated in the cupola, staring out to sea.

Bill and Shelly Conway purchased the captain's mansion in June 1988. "It was derelict, basically on its last legs. It had been a restaurant for over fifty years, and it was supposed to be turnkey, but it wasn't." Shelly recalls that even its name was a

The cupola where Rebecca's ghost maintains her vigil.

misunderstanding. "Our realtor told us he was taking us to see the Captain's alehouse. As soon as we heard that, we said, 'We are not interested in an alehouse.' The real estate agent got flustered, and said, 'No, no, no. It's not the *ale*house, it's the *Linnell* house, and it's a fine dining restaurant.' My husband, Bill, is a master chef, and I am a restoration gardener, so we were happy we weren't going to see a tavern, but still the place was a disappointment. It was so overgrown it looked haunted."

When asked if she was aware of any stories about the mansion, Shelly jumps right in. "Ghosts? When we first came here there truly was a ghost. There was a sense of coldness when you walked from room to room. We lived upstairs over the restaurant with

The stairs lead to the Conways' private quarters.

our four kids. My youngest had just turned four, so I would walk around here at all hours of the night. There would be a sense that somebody had just left the room. You would see a door close, a curtain flutter as if someone passed by. It wasn't frightening—it was more like sadness."

Shelly sighs as her eyes are drawn to the logs crackling in the huge fireplace in the ballroom. She turns back with a smile. "As we fixed it up, the sadness got less and less. We had been here about ten years, and I was up about two-thirty in the morning, and I can remember realizing the coldness was gone. There was more of a sense of warmth, like total acceptance, appreciative that we had loved and cared for this house again." Shelly feels that the house is now as romantic for her and her husband as it was for its original owners.

The Conways have created an enchanting ambiance, hosting intimate dinners, elegant parties, and treasured weddings. They also have reestablished a lovely custom. Based on some of Rebecca's letters, Shelly learned that it was the captain's habit to send his bride roses. "We always have pink roses. That's our trademark because it's the particular flower Rebecca loved." The Conways order upwards of five dozen roses a week and collect all of the petals because "people like to throw them at the weddings."

At one blissful affair, there were more than scattered petals left behind. "After that particular wedding, a guest insisted he saw someone dressed like a bride on the lawn." This would have been a natural sight, says an agreeable Shelly, but "the bride had already left." Attempts were made to mollify the guest. "It was like, okay, okay, and then we sort of questioned him about maybe he had been drinking a little, but he seemed totally sane and rational, except even after we explained that the bride and groom had driven off, he wouldn't let it go. He kept saying, "I just saw her on the front lawn." Shelly believes that he saw a figure in a long, white gown and assumed it was the bride. Could the stunning apparition have been Rebecca drawn to the fragrant roses? For Shelly, that would be a lovely bonus. After all, readers of *Cape Cod*

Rebecca's favorite flowers in the dining room.

Life have voted the Captain Linnell House as the most romantic wedding venue on the Cape.

In addition to the mysterious bride, other diners have reported looking out the windows and seeing people coming up the path from the beach. Again, this is a perfectly ordinary occurrence—with one small caveat. Shelly says that her guests would describe the approaching men as wearing clothing similar to the impeccable style of Captain Linnell. The *Linnell Family Newsletter* also alludes to tales about the captain's ghost "walking the grounds and rooms of the Linnell mansion."

Shelly and Bill Conway fell in love with a sea captain's mansion and bought the once-neglected home on a "young and crazy whim." It appears that it needed them as much as they needed it. Amid the fragrant, sweet smells of trailing wisteria, lavender, and roses, the Captain Linnell House of today nourishes the heart. Eben and Rebecca are reunited; their portraits hang side by side in the inviting lobby of this premier Cape Cod restaurant. "This is a happy place to work. And, to continue making people feel good and giving them a place to create special moments is an honor."

Lagniappe: Capt. Eben Linnell was reputed to be unequaled among American ship masters for native ability, energy, and

Rebecca and Eben, reunited at the Captain Linnell House.

shrewdness. In 1855, he raced his most famous clipper ship, the Massachusetts-built *Eagle Wing,* from London to Hong Kong in 83½ days, a record that still stands. While at home in a rare lull between voyages, he invented an improved top-sail rig, which was patented and incorporated in the design of sixty-four ships. A scale model of the *Eagle Wing* is on display in the enclosed garden dining room, a former terrace. The Conways are delighted to have been able to preserve a part of Cape Cod history. Chef Bill Conway oversees the kitchen, turning out classic American cuisine, and Shelly oversees the front of house and the lush gardens. Shelly holds a picture of the house as it looked in 1852. "Where we are sitting in the ballroom was the barn. The passageway between our ballroom and the lobby was a carriage house and shed. If you are standing in the lobby, you are actually standing in the original Cape Codder. All the way to the left is the French villa addition, now our fine dining spaces." Shelly feels that it must have been particularly hard for Rebecca to finish the villa by herself, as her husband died before it was completed. This may account for the sadness Shelly sensed when she and her family first moved into the captain's house. Perhaps it stemmed from a previous owner, who died after a long addiction to alcohol. Shelly and Bill conclude their recap of the house's history on a lighter note. "I think something that stands out in my mind was when Matt Damon came here for his college roommate's wedding. All he did was stand out back and talk to the kitchen help, and for the last dance, he danced with his roommate's grandmother. He was a really great guy," says Bill. Shelly is next. "One of the restaurant owners before us would go down to the beach and dress up like Lady Godiva. So, we have had some colorful characters pass through here."

7

The Single-Minded Spirit of a Sea Captain's Granddaughter

The spectral figure hovers in the sun-filled bedchamber where she was born and died. Unsettled, she whirls around, seeking something familiar. The spirit of Julia Warren Swift Wood floats out into the hall and enters a second bedchamber, one a bit more to her liking.

The ghostly female form plucks a decorative hair comb off the vanity and attempts to stick it in her upswept locks. It won't hold; it tumbles to the floor. Frustrated, she moves on. A small shriek of delight escapes from her lips. In the corner is her grandmother's treasured parasol, with its whalebone handle. On the mantel are seashells and bits of coral, souvenirs that her grandfather, whaling captain Warren Bourne, collected on his travels to the Seychelles and other exotic ports around the world.

Julia remembers too late not to touch or move anything. She rushes to retrieve the hair comb off the worn rug where it has fallen but struggles to recall its exact placement. She knows that when the tours of the 1790 Dr. Francis Wicks House museum start in the morning, the docents will question who entered the house after it was locked for the day.

Julia shakes her head over her hampered movements in her former domicile. She throws her hands up in mock surrender, nearly knocking a porcelain teacup off its saucer. She settles the wobbling cup and flies out of the room.

In the hall, she passes a pale green, pine, blanket chest and silently thanks her niece's husband for thoughtfully returning it, along with a gold mirror. The memory is bittersweet. Julia had bequeathed

Julia's spirit has an itch to inspect her former home.
(Courtesy Falmouth Historical Society)

the items to her niece, and they had only come back following her niece's death. She'd like to blame the docents for putting the blanket chest in the wrong place, but how were they to know where it rightfully belongs?

Julia glides down the staircase, choosing to ignore the nineteenth-century French wallpaper. The passage of time is virtually meaningless in the spirit world, but she is fairly certain that some well-meaning soul in the late 1940s thought it was a good idea to install the wallpaper that originally hung in another house in town. In Julia's mind, the classic flourishes of the paper clash with the simple "four rigger" layout of her home.

Julia's ghost refrains from crossing the threshold of the front room at the foot of the staircase. She finds the restored medical office of the original owner, Dr. Francis Wicks, with its surgical instruments and bottles of potions, a little unnerving. She itches to sneak in and hide the photo of a child with its sad face pockmarked with smallpox pustules. She'd stuck it in a drawer more than once before, but each time the misplaced photo created a big stir among the docents until it was found and returned to a place of prominence on the doctor's desk.

The dining room is confusing. In Julia's time it was two small rooms. Now the dividing walls have been removed to form one large exhibit space. In this expansive area, a recessed archway showcases blue and white porcelain dishes. It's not that she minds the display; it's again just not her taste.

She gravitates instead to a drop-leaf table that showcases her silver tea set. She begins, as is her daily custom, to wipe off any errant smudges. When a docent points out the monogrammed *S* (for Julia's maiden name of Swift), there is always someone on the tour who simply has to touch or, worse, trace the letter with a fingertip. Julia's spirit follows discretely behind each group, clutching a lace handkerchief for smudge removal. The trick is in the timing, so that no one on the tour inadvertently spots the cloth moving back and forth by itself.

Being a ghost has it challenges. Hiding in the shadows is the

Julia's ghost polishes her silver tea set.

preferred modus operandi. However, there are occasions when it becomes necessary to pop in and gently correct an obvious error. Julia wishes she could explain to the museum's board of directors that she doesn't like causing trouble, and she surely doesn't want to draw attention to herself, but certain things need a nudge . . . or two.

James would have understood. Julia married James Wood in 1873. He was thirty-five; she was twenty-four. Both had attained a sufficient maturity of years to sustain a companionable marriage for twenty-seven years. The death of their infant son, Clifton, and James' death in 1900 were the two tragedies that haunt her still.

As a widow and now childless mother, Julia grappled with finding a purpose for her life. Through her mother, Sophia Bourne

Julia's husband, James Wood.
(Courtesy Falmouth Historical Society)

Swift (married to Benjamin Palmer Swift), Julia had inherited the home of her grandfather, Capt. Warren Bourne. Following the death of her mother and husband James, Julia moved back to the home on Palmer Avenue. The preservation of the yellow house, with its widow's walk and Greek Revival porch, became an obsession that continues in her afterlife. Although Julia Warren

Warren Nye Bourne, Julia's grandfather. (Courtesy Falmouth Historical Society)

The graves of Julia and James Wood at the Oak Grove Cemetery in Falmouth.

Swift Wood is buried next to James in Falmouth's Oak Grove Cemetery, her spirit has a certain wanderlust.

Julia cherishes her memories and has a tendency to rearrange. Docents are kept busy returning items to their correct placement within the rooms; they'd like to believe it is just a curious visitor touching what is not allowed. Or when doors are flung open, rational minds blame it on a gust of wind, faulty hinges, a distracted docent.

Julia left her grandfather's home to be preserved by the Falmouth Historical Society, and they in turn named it the Julia Wood House. Although honored by the gesture, Julia's spirit bristles because they ignored her wishes. In her will, she'd made it quite clear that the donation of the house was to be "in memory of her grandfather Capt. Warren Nye Bourne." For the Society to have rechristened it the 1790 Dr. Francis Wicks House was disconcerting. Yes, Julia is willing to acknowledge that Dr. Wicks built it in 1790, and yes, the good doctor advocated for smallpox inoculations for all his patients. Still she'd prefer the home be called the Captain Warren Bourne House.

What caused the ghost of Julia to reemerge? She'd been sleeping peacefully next to James in the nearby cemetery for well over a century and a half. Did the incessant pounding of hammers, the buzz of power tools, and the presence of a horde of workers as repairs and renovations were done in 2019 pique Julia's need to oversee the ongoing evolution of her home? If so, with a little tweak here and there, Julia's spirit is ensuring that the legacy of

Julia's former home, where her spirit tidies up.

her family, the Bournes and the Swifts, remains front and center at the 1790 Dr. Francis Wicks House museum.

Lagniappe: Julia Warren Swift Wood died in 1932. In her will, she bequeathed her home to the Falmouth Historical Society. She also unwittingly left them with a $10,000 debt. Due to Julia's lengthy illness and a dwindling legacy, there was an outstanding mortgage on the property. Fortunately, the Society began its first capital campaign and successfully raised the necessary funds to clear title to the property. The Falmouth Historical Society's Museums on the Green complex has grown to a two-acre campus showcasing two historic homes (the Wicks and Conant houses), a barn, cultural center, and ancillary structures surrounded by gardens and woods. Visitors are welcome. As for the obsessive spirit of the last private occupant, Julia Warren Swift Wood, granddaughter of sea captain Warren Bourne, no one on the present board of directors objects to a single-minded ghost's tendency to tidy up.

The haunted façade of the Penniman House in Eastham.

8

The House on the Hill in Eastham

"I came to see the ghost." Michael, nine years old, dressed in a red Patriots sweatshirt and faded jeans, is on a mission. Standing in the doorway of the Edward Penniman House in Eastham, his head pivots rapidly to the right and left, up and down. Michael's mother apologizes to the tour guide on duty. "He found an old copy of the book *The Ghost at the Penniman House* at my sister's house in Wellfleet, and he begged me to bring him here." The male volunteer stares blankly back at the woman and her son. Michael's mother tries again. "It's a children's book about a little girl who sees a ghost digging in the garden at Penniman House." The elderly guide scratches at his neck and squints at Michael, who is shifting from one foot to the other, impatient to get inside. "Don't know about any ghost, but come on in."

Michael and his parents peer into the dimly lit space of the roped-off parlor, displaying its original Penniman-family furniture. The inquisitive boy is disappointed that he can't step inside and explore. The guide quickly assures him that he is free to roam the rest of the house, and Michael bounds up the stairs. He stomps back down a few minutes later, announcing that there is nothing up there.

Michael is partially correct. This former whaling captain's home is sparsely furnished. The majority of the artifacts were sold at auction prior to its acquisition by the National Park Service in 1963. The last occupant was Irma Broun, the granddaughter of Capt. Edward Penniman, who built the mansion in 1868. Because the park lacked the funds to properly seal the environment, it has

Capt. Edward Penniman, seated in the parlor. (Photograph courtesy National Park Service)

been swept clean of most of the personal touches. Visiting hours are limited to one afternoon a week. The house, with its washed-out red mansard roof, sits like a lonely old spinster sequestered from the rest of humanity. Its very isolation fuels its haunted reputation. A repeat visitor from Maryland concurs: "I've been to the old whaling captain's home and always get a strange feeling of sadness and a sense of being watched."

If the visitor was referring to the ghost of Captain Penniman, he likely would have found a very imposing apparition. E. G. Perry, in his 1898 book *A Trip Around Cape Cod,* described Penniman as "that arctic whaleman . . . a man whose record Cape Cod history will not let die." The captain's obituary read: "With his stalwart physique and commanding features, he looked every inch the sea captain of romance in the days of Cape Cod's prominence on the seas."

The damp sea air trails through the house and carries with it a foreboding chill. Visitors glance warily over their shoulders. In the late summer of 2013, in the final days before the home is boarded up for the long winter season ahead, a young couple from Connecticut hurries through the rooms. Their final stop is the parlor. "It feels like he's following us, as if he wants to make sure we don't touch any of his things." The husband towers over his wife and tells her that she is being paranoid. The young woman tugs at the bottom of her navy blue sweater and wraps the loose ends more tightly around her waist. "Seriously, did you look at the captain's picture? Those eyes—those are ghost eyes. This place is haunted. And it's not a friendly ghost, so it can't be his daughter, Bessie, even if she did die in the house. You heard the guide. He said she loved living here, so it's not her following us around. It's the captain. He wants the place to himself."

Long-time volunteer Shirley Sabin wishes that people would focus more on the history of Penniman House instead of on the ghosts. "Some people say that the house is haunted or that there are spirits in the house—depends on who you are talking to." She feels these rumors might have started when it was boarded up for a number of years. "When the park got it, they didn't do anything with it until a grant was funded, and then they decided to restore it." Nor did it help that when the house was used as a temporary residence for park rangers, the rangers and their families began to speak about ghosts inside. "There is a story about a ranger and his wife who were living there," says Sabin, "and they claimed things would happen, nothing bad, just things would get moved, or they would hear things, and then the rumors were 'Oh, it's the Captain. Oh, it's Mrs. Penniman. Oh, it's Bessie.'"

Besides the captain, the second ghost candidate is the captain's wife, Betsey Augusta Knowles Penniman. Adventurous, brave, and loyal, she sailed around the world with her husband, including on a four-year voyage on the whaling bark *Minerva*. "Gustie," the captain's nickname for his wife, took over command when nature and necessity dictated. The Pennimans' daughter, Bessie, wrote of one instance when her mother's navigational skills saved the ship. "When Captain Penniman and most of the crew were ashore off Patagonia, South America, suddenly a tropical storm arose, and the ship was blown one hundred miles out to sea. Under her direction, the *Europa* weathered the storm at sea and returned two days later, with all sails set, to pick up Captain Penniman and his crew."

Whether at sea or on land, Gustie Penniman's good humor, even at her own expense, never faltered. She dared to wear a pair of men's pants, taboo for woman of that era, to help her husband repair the keel of their pleasure sailboat, *Elsie*. To mark the occasion, Gustie penned a poem, "For the Dollar Scrabble."

> I said to earn my dollar,
> I would help my charming spouse,
> But he as quick retorted
> That my place was in the house.
> . . .
> But I donned a tam "shanter"
> And bloomers neat and natty
> While my daughter was convulsed with glee,
> and my husband called me fatty.

With such a jovial outlook, Gustie's spirit surely appreciates each and every visitor and takes all their comments in stride.

Gustie and Edward Penniman had three children: Eugene, born in 1860; Betsey ("Bessie"), born in 1868; and Edward ("Ned"), born in 1870. They all spent time at sea with their parents. While the boys fared well, Bessie suffered from seasickness. In a letter to his daughter, Captain Penniman acknowledged that life on a whaling ship is not always pleasant:

Dear Bessie,
It is a dark stormy day. . . I don't think you would enjoy yourself at

sea, and I see by your writing that you don't care to come. You will be much better off going to school . . . than you would on board the *Jacob A. Howland*. . . . We did catch a very large right whale the other day. The *Jacob* does not smell very sweet. I expect you would snuff up your nose if you was here and say she did not smell good . . . Hope this will find you well and happy.
Papa

Bessie stayed with her aunt in Cambridge, returning home only when her family had safely arrived from exotic ports from the Arctic Ocean to the South Pacific. Bessie is the third possible candidate for the ghost who lives at Penniman House.

The Pennimans' home in Eastham was built on land in the Fort Hill area, where Captain Penniman had grown up. The two-and-a-half-story Second Empire-style structure rises over a raised terrace. From the octagonal cupola, the family could gaze at the Atlantic Ocean and Cape Cod Bay. The Pennimans' granddaughter described the early twentieth century view:

> We had a beautiful view of the town Cove, the ocean and the sand dunes. . . . The sun rising out of the sea was spectacular. We watched whales blow as they swam and cavorted in the water, as seen from our dining room window. Now all that is gone as the trees have been allowed to grow.

At fifty-three, Captain Penniman retired from whaling and settled into the life of a gentleman farmer in his new home, built on twelve acres of land, with barns, greenhouse, orchard, gardens, and outbuildings. The eight-room home was said to be the first on the Cape with indoor plumbing. There was a three-hole outhouse attached to the barn for servants and laborers.

The captain died in 1913, leaving the house to his wife, Gustie. Their sons married and moved on. Daughter Bessie may have never truly left. "Bessie lived there her entire eighty-nine years," explains Sabin. "Bessie never married, never had children."

Surrounded by the artifacts her parents had collected—scrimshaw, china tea sets, Cloisonné vases—Bessie, who inherited the house in 1921, clung to the memories, never changing or moving anything from its appointed place. This may explain why some who believe the house has ghosts assume it is Bessie's spirit. Upset that family treasures and mementos are missing and can't be found, the ghostly form of Bessie roams from room to room. Occasional reports surface of a lone female figure carrying a kerosene lamp. She appears in one window and then moves on to the next.

However, while Bessie never had children, she was not childless. Bessie's younger brother, Ned, had three daughters. After the death of his wife, the older girls went to live with other relatives, and the youngest, two-year-old Irma, moved in with her grandparents and aunt. Aunt Bessie raised Irma, who is the fourth possibility for the ghost. Like her Aunt Bessie, Irma developed a strong attachment and protectiveness toward her childhood home.

According to Sabin, who researched the Penniman family history, "Irma lived there with her Aunt Bessie until she married at twenty-one or twenty-two." Irma's first marriage and subsequent divorce is a mystery. "The previous head of the park's Visitor Center interviewed Irma and made a tape. Irma talked about her life, that she had been married in the parlor. It was a short marriage that didn't work out." Sabin is puzzled. "I can't find any records, no marriage certificate in town. I don't know who the man was."

What is known is that by the summer of 1932, Irma was single again and living back at Penniman House. Irma volunteered at Cape Cod's Ornithological Research Station, where she met ornithologist Maurice Broun. Irma, not one for shyness, recognized her soul mate immediately and walked right up to him. "I think it would be great to marry an ornithologist," she said. Irma got her way. "They fell in love," says Sabin, "and Maurice later wrote a book, and he talked about how Irma would go with him to these smelly, dirty rookeries, and how if she could put up with all this and bird banding, then he would band her.

So, they married, and he was absolutely the love of her life." Irma became Mrs. Maurice Broun in 1934 and moved with her husband to the Hawk Mountain Sanctuary in Pennsylvania, but Penniman House and Aunt Bessie were always in her thoughts.

Even when Aunt Bessie was living in the house, its outward appearance instilled in visitors a sense of foreboding. In his memoir, *The Autobiography of a Yankee-Nevadan,* George A. Phelps describes the 1944 trip he took with Irma to check up on her elderly aunt, who "lived in the house that belonged to her father, a turn-of-the-century Yankee sea captain who had sailed the seven seas." Phelps says that they arrived on a spooky Halloween night.

> Mist, rising from the nearby bay swirled around us as we walked beneath a Gothic arch, the jawbones of a whale. I shivered, not only because of the chilly night air but also because the place looked as it was haunted. I half expected to be greeted by witches and hobgoblins.

As they approached the front entrance, George's misgivings increased. "With a squeak, the door swung open to reveal a small, gray-haired lady holding a shawl over her sloping shoulders. Aunt Bessie fondly greeted her niece and then held out a thin, pale hand to me." To the uneasy guest, the interior, "looking more a museum than a dwelling," offered little to lessen his discomfort. "There were more foreign artifacts and exotic memorabilia than I'd ever before seen in one place."

Bessie Penniman died at the Penniman House. In her will, she left the house and its contents to the local cemetery association in the hopes that they would continue to care for the Penniman family plot. There was one important proviso—Irma and her husband were to have a lifetime tenancy. Irma, however, was not happy with the arrangement. She approached the cemetery association and, after a prolonged negotiation, purchased the title to Penniman House. Although Irma and Maurice did vacation there, the couple's primary residence remained in Pennsylvania.

Irma continued to worry about the future of her childhood home.

The Cape Cod National Seashore was established in 1961. Irma offered the home to them with the idea that it would be opened as a museum. The park service wanted this prime piece of land to save it from development but had little interest in the house—or its contents. "Irma offered to sell the furniture for an additional one hundred dollars a room, which would have been an absolute gold mine," states Sabin. "The man she was dealing with said to her, 'We are not in the antique business.' She was so hurt. This is directly from her mouth because I communicated with her for several years before she died."

Because she could not be there to care for the Penniman House, the sale to the National Park Service went through, and Irma had no other option but to put her family heirlooms on the auction block. For the first time in three generations, the Penniman House would be vacant, boarded up and devoid of life. The rumors of a haunted house on the hill resurfaced.

Maurice Broun, Irma's husband, died of cancer in 1979. To great surprise, Irma soon wed husband number three: Spencer Kahn, Maurice's best man at his wedding to Irma. Once married, Spencer Kahn and Irma Broun moved to Kahn's home in Modesto, California.

After its short stint as temporary housing for park rangers, the National Park Service opened Penniman House to tours on a limited basis. When Shirley and her husband, Ed Sabin, began to volunteer as tour guides, they contacted Irma Penniman Broun Kahn in California. "At the time, very little was known or written down about family. I have a very curious mind, and if we were going to do tours, we needed to learn more."

Irma, widowed once again, invited the Sabins to California for a visit. Irma died a week before their much-anticipated meeting. She was ninety-seven. Irma's accountant called to say that he saw the date of the meeting on the calendar—it was important to Irma, and she would have wanted them notified. "I asked when was the service, and we went," states Sabin. "It was the shortest service I have ever been to in my entire life. Irma had said [to] keep it short, but I don't think she meant that short!"

The accountant shocked the Sabins even further when he asked if they would take Irma's ashes back to the Penniman House and put them on the mantle. "I said, 'I don't think so.'" Sabin just couldn't imagine Irma's ashes in an urn perched on the fireplace mantel in an empty house. She had a better idea. "I suggested he bury the ashes in the Penniman family plot. In fact, I told him that her name is already on the big headstone along with Maurice's." Sabin added, "If you want to do that, I will arrange a memorial service and write the eulogy." Local family members attended, along with Irma's accountant and a staff member from Hawk Mountain. "So, we had all aspects of her life represented, including representatives of the cemetery association. We buried her ashes. Maurice's had been scattered. We put a stone with Irma's name. She always said she wanted to go home, and home was Eastham, where she grew up."

Three generations of Pennimans—the captain and his wife, Gustie; their children, Eugene, Edward, Bessie; and their granddaughter, Irma Penniman Broun Kahn—lived in and loved the Penniman House. If Capt. Edward Penniman's spirit is watching over the house, Sabin agrees that he would probably be pleased that the National Park is allowing visitors to enter, but "he would want them to keep it in better shape—I am sure that's true." She adds, "I expect he would like to have it furnished, but that is not possible."

One ghost or four? An accurate tally of the spirits of the Penniman House is left to the individual. "I've had strangers come into the house and they'd say that they feel things. The wife of one of our rangers, one of our volunteers, doesn't like to be there. Our curator, who is retired, didn't like to go over there; she didn't like the vibe she gets." Shirley Sabin, the eighty-year-old tour guide, has had no issues with the house and remains a skeptic.

Lagniappe: To find the Penniman House, head towards Eastham

The entrance to the Penniman House is through the jawbones of a whale.

on Route 6A. Turn right on Fort Hill Road and follow its serpentine pathway. Drive past the captain's house on the right. The parking lot is at the bottom of the next hill on the left. Climb back up on foot and enter the grounds through the side "gate." Walk beneath the mammoth, bleached-white jaw bones of a sixty-three-foot whale, and you will feel a bit like George Phelps when he arrived on Halloween eve in 1944. The jaws have served as the main entrance since the days of Captain Penniman—a stark reminder of his source of wealth and days at sea.

The Provincetown library, home to the Rose Dorothea.

9

A Clean Sweep

The *Rose Dorothea* rides under full sail on the second floor of the Provincetown library. The schooner measures sixty-six feet six inches long, and her forty-eight-foot main mast skims the third floor ceiling. She is the largest indoor boat model of her kind and has one other notable distinction: the *Rose Dorothea* is skippered by a phantom captain.

The Provincetown library occupies a stunning 1860s-era edifice on Commercial Street. In the third-floor loft, a library patron works diligently at his laptop. On a clear summer day, the towering windows offer an expansive view, stretching some fifteen miles over the harbor and bay, but the eyes of graduate student John never veer from his computer monitor. After two grueling hours, John allows himself a short break. He removes his black, wire-frame reading glasses and lays them over the keyboard. He pinches the bridge of his nose and rubs his eyes. Mid-rub, he freezes and then slowly rotates his shoulders clockwise to stare down at the deck of the *Rose Dorothea*. With his head cocked slightly, John appears to be listening. The silence is broken abruptly by his loud laughter. A librarian, pushing a cart stacked with books past the hull, frowns in disapproval. Waving his hand in acknowledgement of his transgression, John mouths a perfunctory "I'm sorry."

When asked what made him laugh so hard, John is unabashed. "I just can't help it. When I hear the sweep—the *swish, swish, swish* of that broom—I mean, what more of a motivator can you ask for? It's as if he knows I need a push to get to the finish line." John is quick to clarify. "It's Captain Perry, of course—his spirit,

The bow of the replica of the Rose Dorothea *under the third-floor loft.*

A phantom captain sweeps the deck with a phantom broom.

anyway. John underscores the connection between himself and the former captain of the *Rose Dorothea*. "I know it could seem strange listening for ghosts and ghost brooms in a library, but ever since I started coming here to work on my master's thesis about sailing vessels in New England waters, well, I'm just aware he's here, and he approves, and it's his way of helping."

Capt. Marion Perry is hailed as the winner of the 1907 Fisherman's Cup sailing race, a forty-two-mile dash between Boston to Gloucester and back also known as the Lipton Cup. As his fishing schooner crossed the finish line, Captain Perry is said to have grabbed a broom and "swept the deck clean," a symbolic gesture of having beaten his rival, the *Jessie Costa*, captained by Manuel Costa. During the June 25, 1988, dedication ceremony for the replica of the *Rose Dorothea,* a Portuguese man, boat builder Francis "Flyer" Santos, also grabbed a broom and "swept the deck" in emulation of Captain Perry, who brought fame to his homeport of Provincetown.

The original *Rose Dorothea* was a Grand Banks fishing schooner with a rounded Indian Head bow that enabled her to sail closer to the wind, making her faster than other schooners of her era. Built in 1905 at a cost of $15,000, she measured just more than 108 feet in length. The captain named her for his lovely wife.

The library's replica clearly honors Captain Perry's victory, but it is just a showpiece. Her hull gleams in the sunlight with a glossy coat of black paint. Not a speck of dirt mars her pristine, white deck. Her name glistens in gold script on her bow. It would be reasonable to question why Captain Perry's ghost would haunt a replica rather than his actual ship.

The schooner met a horrific end. Sold in 1910 to a local fishing captain, six years later she was sold again to a Newfoundland company that used her to ferry salt and supplies to Portugal. In February 1917, a German submarine surfaced next to the schooner. After allowing her crew to evacuate in dories, the U-boat sank her. This once-valiant fishing vessel disintegrated at the bottom of the sea off the coast of Portugal. So, with nothing left of his ship to command, Captain Perry's invincible spirit seems to have chosen the library's magnificent half-scale model to relive his victory in the great Fisherman's Cup race.

The race began on August 1, 1907, in Boston. The *Rose Dorothea* and the *Jessie Costa,* another Provincetown schooner, battled to steal the wind from the other's sails. A third vessel, the *James W. Parker,* reputedly with a band on board, lagged behind. As the *Rose Dorothea* and the *Jessie Costa* rounded Gloucester for the return leg back to Boston, the rising wind and seas pushed the boats faster, "heeling them over so their rails were tipped to the water line." Approaching the final mark, the crew of the *Rose Dorothea* heard a sharp crack. The foretopmast had snapped in the middle, leaving its sail to dangle uselessly. The jubilant crew of the *Jessie Costa* was eager to take advantage of their competitor's disaster—but fate and skillful sailing intervened. Without its jib topsail, the *Rose Dorothea* could point higher into the wind and sail a straighter course. The *Jessie Costa* had to tack more often. The *Rose Dorothea,* minus its foretopmast, crossed the finish line two minutes and thirty-four seconds ahead of its closest competitor. As she entered Boston harbor, Captain Perry grabbed a broom, swept the deck clean, and celebrated with a flourish. If the captain's spirit is still at it, who can blame him? The library is accessible to all, and sometimes even ghosts appreciate a little attention.

Captain Perry's prize was $650 and the Lipton Cup, a three-foot-tall sterling-silver trophy. Presenting the Lipton Cup to the sea captain was then-mayor of Boston John F. "Honey Fitz" Fitzgerald, the grandfather of Pres. John F. Kennedy and United States senators Robert "Bobby" Kennedy and Edward "Ted" Kennedy.

Perry brought the Lipton Cup back to Provincetown, where today it has a place of honor inside the library's main entrance. A majestic eagle perches on top of the ornate trophy. A pair of winged seahorses serves as handles. Other symbols of the sea—embossed sea shells, whimsical fish—adorn the sides. In 1980, the trophy was stolen and held for a $2,000 ransom. The bumbling thief was already a suspect in several similar crimes, and the

Lipton Cup soon was recovered from where it had been hastily stashed in nearby sand dunes. After a thorough cleaning, it was back on display with the engraving on the ebony base proclaiming: "Presented by Sir Thomas Lipton, 1907, and won by the schooner *Rose Dorothea.*"

Who was this knighted British gentleman, and why would he sponsor a race between fishermen in Massachusetts waters?

Having made three failed attempts to win the coveted America's Cup for Great Britain, this millionaire mogul of tea fame earned the title of "World's Best Loser." Sir Thomas Lipton sought to redeem himself, and he was not above a bit of clever marketing. The founder of the Lipton Tea Company, he was involved with branding before branding ever entered the advertising lexicon. Tired of racing fabulously expensive pleasure yachts owned by like-minded gentlemen, Sir Thomas looked for a new diversion. Intrigued by the speed and seaworthiness of New England's commercial fishing fleet, he offered a custom-made trophy to the winner of a coastal race where "winds were unpredictable, and sail and helm handling were crucial elements to success." The Lipton Cup featured enameled flags of the United States and England. A closer look reveals a smaller flag with a green shamrock in the center, a crafty way of incorporating the flags of Lipton's three *Shamrock*s, the yachts which Lipton had sailed in pursuit of his thwarted America's Cup dream.

When Lipton first approached Perry about participating in the Fisherman's Race, the frugal captain declined. The price of fish was soaring, and a frivolous sailing race held little appeal. However, the captain's wife, Rose Dorothea, who "favored nice things," had a different agenda. Once she glimpsed the extravagant trophy, she knew that the only proper place for it was on her parlor mantel. The big, barrel-chested captain, sporting a reputation as the "best fish-killer" in the fleet, acquiesced to the desire of his wife. With her husband's amazing win, Rose Dorothea's mantel had a shiny new centerpiece, and Provincetown's seafaring reputation as the best of the best was secured.

In the early 1900s, Provincetown remained primarily a fishing village. The victory made Perry a local hero, allowed the largely Portuguese population to "rise above the ethnic slurs flung their way," and erased the smug superiority of nearby Gloucester, which was known for building fast fishing schooners. It also one-upped Boston, where society's elite raced yachts that often cost more than an entire fishing crew made in its lifetime.

The *Provincetown (MA) Advocate*, a local newspaper, touted the triumphant homecoming of Captain Perry aboard the *Rose Dorothea*: "Volleys were fired from small arms by men stationed at intervals along the route . . . [the] good-natured crowd voiced their approval in cheers for the skillful captain, his doughty crew, and the trim hull that successfully fought for the grandest racing trophy known in fishing annals the world over."

Given the impact of the race on his hometown, his pride in his Portuguese heritage, and the admiration of his wife, it is understandable that Capt. Marion Perry's ghost still has an itch to gloat. This is, after all, the ghost of a man who, when Pres. Theodore Roosevelt was in Boston and wanted to meet the Lipton Cup winner, is reported to have responded: "Tell the President if he wants to see me, he knows where he can find me!"

For patrons of the Provincetown library such as graduate student John, it's not hard to find the captain's steadfast spirit. Those believers are just as certain that the *swish, swish, swish* of the phantom broom across the deck of the reborn *Rose Dorothea* is the captain's little reminder to steer for the stars.

Lagniappe: There are some interesting questions about this entire situation: What is a ship's model of this magnitude doing inside a library, and how did it get there in the first place? The current Provincetown library began life as the Center Methodist Episcopal Church. At its completion in 1860, it was the largest church building of the Methodist denomination anywhere in the United States. It eventually proved to be too big for the congregation, and in 1958, the Methodists sold the church with its one-hundred-foot

The deck of the replica with its phantom captain and broom.

Ovals were cut into the ceiling to accommodate the masts.

spire to Walter P. Chrysler Jr. for an art museum. The venture failed, as did a 1974 attempt to create a "Center for the Arts." On July 4, 1976, it reopened as the Provincetown Heritage Museum. The museum's board needed an attraction that would be a tourist draw, and a model of the *Rose Dorothea* fulfilled their vision of the ultimate symbol of Provincetown's glory days of sailing and fishing. Master boat builder Francis "Flyer" Santos, the grandson of one of the original crew, was hired to build a half-scale replica. Mimicking the model-ship-in-a-bottle technique, Santos constructed the *Rose Dorothea* replica from the hull up using the former second-floor church sanctuary as a permanent

The library repurposed church pews for their bookshelves.

dry dock. Though half-scale, the replica's size required a few structural modifications to the building.

Ovals were cut into the ceiling to accommodate the height of the masts. The special glass doors of the aptly named Bowsprit Reading Room (the former choir loft) were designed to allow the ship's protruding bowsprit to point towards the harbor. The exacting process took eleven years. On June 25, 1988, the completed model was dedicated to the fishermen of Provincetown and their remarkable sailing schooners. By 2000, as museum visitors declined, use of the old Provincetown library increased, and the collections of the two institutions merged. The *Rose Dorothea,* the victorious fishing schooner, remains the soaring centerpiece of the library. Bookshelves in the form of waves follow the curve of the hull. To pay homage to the building's ecclesiastical origins, mahogany arm rests from the former church pews are now decorative caps for display shelves on the first floor. The church bells in the belfry still ring—instead of calling congregants to prayer, they announce the daily opening of the library doors and the opportunity to view the *Rose Dorothea,* whose phantom captain stands alert at the helm to inspire and encourage.

10

A Whale of a Tale

Poised with lance in hand, the second mate of the whaleship *Congress* went for the kill. But the wounded whale abruptly turned and struck the boat. Young Caleb's feet were tangled in the line intended to drag the whale. Yanked overboard, he plummeted some fifty feet into the waters off Australia. Caleb Osborn Hamblin's leg was caught inside the cavernous jaws of a sperm whale.

Caleb Osborn Hamblin, with his signature mustache. (Courtesy Falmouth Historical Society)

In his genealogical history of the Hamblin family, Henry Franklin Andrews described the horrific incident: "On May 12, 1858, three boats had made fast to the whale. It fought, knocking the captain and another male overboard, and then attacked Hamblin's boat, opening and closing its twenty-two foot long jaws with great force. The whale struck the boat and threw Hamblin astride its lower jaw with his leg in the corner of its mouth. It then dove into the sea, as Hamblin remarked 'with a sorry mouthful.'" Andrews concluded the harrowing tale with a whopper of a twist: "Retaining his presence of mind, he [Hamblin] clung to a line made fast to the boat and was literally torn out of the whale's mouth, rose to the surface, and was taken into the boat in time to deal a death blow with his lance to the whale."

Caleb O. Hamblin's survivor's tale became the source of legend and is noted throughout Cape Cod and maritime histories.

Escaping the jaws of a whale was not Hamblin's only brush with death at sea. On a voyage in 1853 off the Crozet Islands, he harpooned a large whale, which slammed the boat and threw him overboard. Caleb managed to scramble back in the boat, and the whale was captured. In February 1854, off the Desolation Islands, the boats made fast to a large whale when another whale came up under his boat, sending it with all six crewmembers into the air and then the sea. Four of the crew managed to climb on top of the boat. One sailor, who did not know how to swim, began to sink. According to reports, Caleb, an expert swimmer, dove down, caught him by the hair, and brought him to the surface. The frightened man nearly drowned Caleb and himself by clinging too tightly around the neck of his rescuer. On subsequent voyages that he captained, bad weather nearly drove his ship ashore into the rocks off New Zealand, and his vessel struck ice in the Arctic Ocean and sprang a leak. His last voyage on the *Trobridge* was also headed for disaster when it was first hit by a hurricane off of Patagonia. Repaired and back out at sea, the ship was struck by another gale, and finally, on Caleb's return from a three-year unsuccessful voyage off the Grand Banks, the *Trobridge* was hit by a tornado that carried away its sails and masts. Through it all, Capt. Caleb Osborn Hamblin persevered.

So it comes as no surprise that Caleb's ghost is also a survivor. The sea captain died at home, a landlubber, at the age of seventy-two. Having overcome more than this share of perils at sea during his lifetime, the captain's ghost (to paraphrase an army ballad about old soldiers) offers proof that old sailors never really die (nor do their ghosts); they just fade away. The apparition of the captain has been spotted fading in and out at his former home in Falmouth on the Cape. Those who've managed to catch a glimpse of the ghost say they recognize Captain Hamblin by his trademark

Caleb retired to this home in West Falmouth, where his spirit keeps watch.

The captain's ghost has been spotted on the front porch.

thick mustache. The front porch is a favorite haunt for the specter of the captain, planting his feet and adopting a wide stance as he would on the deck of a ship. He looks out at the horizon and surveys the passing of the changing world before him.

The captain died April 17, 1907. Visitors to Falmouth's Oak Grove Cemetery claim they've seen a gentleman, formally attired in dress coat and white bowtie, with a wood cane tucked

The phantom of an older gentleman frequents the Hamblin monument in Oak Grove Cemetery.

under his arm, inspecting the pillar that serves as the Hamblin family monument. He will touch his cane to the small marble rolled headstone for his first wife, Emily Robinson Hamblin. The phantom gentleman vanishes as soon as eyes are set on him.

Lagniappe: Whales are mammals; they must come to the surface to breathe air, making them visible to hunters. On whaling vessels, a sailor was sent to the top of the ship's mast to watch for whales. When he spotted the whale exhaling, he would shout to the excited crew below, "She blows!"

Six-man whaleboats were then launched. When they approached the whale, the man nearest the bow stood up and thrust a harpoon attached to a rope into the creature. As the injured whale attempted to swim away, he dragged the whaleboat with him. This terrifying moment was called a "Nantucket sleigh ride."

When the exhausted whale slowed, the officer in the whaleboat delivered the fatal blow with his lance. The whale was then towed back to the ship, where the blubber was cut off with razor-sharp spades. This was when all went well. When it didn't, and the whale proved to be the more formidable opponent, crews were often tossed into the sea and, if lucky, survived to tell the tale.

11

The Pirate and His Would-Be Bride

Two pale figures walk the beach, arms entwined—two lovers, blissfully reunited. From a different perspective, the same male and female apparitions appear locked in a fierce struggle, a pair of angry wraiths driven by revenge. This is a ghostly tale with conflicting outcomes. The legend of the pirate Samuel Bellamy and the elusive Maria Hallett is as controversial today as it was in the spring of 1717 when Bellamy's ship wrecked on the cruel and unforgiving Wellfleet shoals.

Historic records confirm that "Black Sam" Bellamy was a real pirate, not a fictional character. His exploits are well documented. Born in 1689 near Plymouth, in Devonshire, England, his mother, Elizabeth Pain Bellamy, died shortly after Sam's birth. As a young boy, he snuck out to the bustling wharves, captivated by the privateers unloading their wares. Some of Sam's relatives had immigrated to the American colonies and settled in Eastham in Cape Cod, and he joined them in 1714. The unemployed twenty-five-year-old spent his idle hours at the tavern of distant relative Israel Cole on Great Island, across from Wellfleet harbor. The tavern's patrons were a mixed lot: fisherman, whalers, and traders. The tavern was reputed to be a front for a clandestine warehouse where smuggled and stolen goods were bought, stored, and sold, thus evading the bothersome taxes due the English crown.

In the summer of 1715, news of the wreck of a flotilla of Spanish ships off the Florida coast swept through the tavern. The dozen-plus ships, en route to Spain from Havana, carried a cargo of gold coins and bars and chests of silver, emeralds, pearls, and

The ghosts of Maria and Sam–lovers or angry wraiths? (Photograph by Russell Sillery)

Chinese porcelain. Now, this treasure littered the ocean floor in shallow waters—and penniless Sam fantasized about getting his hands on it.

That summer, Sam was also fantasizing about a beautiful young Eastham girl. While there were unsubstantiated rumors that Sam had abandoned a wife and child back in England, here on the lower Cape, Sam's eye settled on Maria Hallett. The most popular version of their initial encounter holds that Maria was sitting in an orchard under a floating white cloud of apple blossoms. Like Eve tempting Adam, the beautiful maiden held forth an apple. The youthful enchantress is described as having hair that "glistened like corn silk at suncoming," and eyes "the color of hyacinth." Reading almost like a modern-day bodice-ripper romance novel, folklorist Elizabeth Reynard recreated the scene of their first tryst in her in her 1930 book *The Narrow Land:* "Black Bellamy made masterful love, sailorman love that remembers how a following wind falls short and makes way while it blows."

The virile, black-haired Lothario and the fifteen-year-old with the golden locks made a dramatic couple. Reynard concluded: "Love was settled between them in no time at all, under the apple tree by the Burying Acre, and Sam sailed away with a promise to Maria that when he returned he would wed her . . . and in a sloop, laden with treasure, carry her back to the Spanish Indies, there to be made princess of a West Indian isle."

The legend of the witch and the pirate was born in an apple orchard in Eastham in the summer of 1715. But who seduced whom? Did Maria bewitch Sam? Is this how the rumor that she was the daughter of a Salem witch began? Or, did he, like the snake in the Garden of Eden, take advantage of a young girl's naïveté and devour the virgin? Whether it was love or lust, the outcome was the same: Maria was pregnant.

Affairs did happen in eighteenth-century Puritan New England. Consummation often preceded the commitment of vows, and estimates for the rate of out-of-wedlock pregnancies approached 25 percent. In 1692, to deal with the economic repercussions of

such situations, Massachusetts passed an act that mandated that
". . . despite his denial, a man who was accused by a woman under
oath at the time of her travail would be adjudged the father of
the child and be responsible for its support with the mother, thus
relieving the town of the child's care."

The same Massachusetts Act of 1692 also punished the fallen
woman. If found guilty of fornication, she was subject to fines
and a public whipping. The issue of an out-of-wedlock pregnancy
could be rectified if it was immediately followed by marriage, not
necessarily to the father of the unborn child. Convention required
a wedding. Maria broke with convention—she would remain
unwed, have her baby, and wait for Sam.

Like the fictional protagonist Hester Prynne in Nathaniel
Hawthorne's novel *The Scarlet Letter,* Maria refused to name the
father of her child. Certainly, her parents, said to be well-to-do
Yarmouth farmers, would have suspected if they had seen Maria
sneaking off to the tavern to be with Sam. They would never have
approved of a man with no prospects.

Sam was also a very persuasive fellow. At the tavern, with
Maria by his side, he hooked up with Palgrave Williams, a man
of means, a jeweler. Williams listened eagerly to Bellamy's get-
rich-quick scheme and offered to procure a ship. Together, they
would scoop up the glittering gold and silver coins lying in the
shallow waters off of Florida. Williams had one stipulation: he
would serve as Quartermaster and be in charge of counting and
dividing equal shares of the anticipated wealth. Of course, they
would be rich beyond their wildest imagination. Bellamy and
Williams assembled a crew in less than three weeks.

The lovers continued their passionate trysts as preparations
were underway. Maria may have shared the secret of her
pregnancy with Sam, which would have provided him with ample
incentive to return quickly. With the gold salvaged from the
wrecked Spanish fleet, he would have abundant wealth to provide
for both Maria and their unborn love child. Since he would be
gone only a few months, she could hide her pregnancy and wait
for his triumphant return.

Bellamy, Williams, and their crew set sail. The months dragged on, and Maria began to show. She could have accepted an offer of marriage from a local farm boy interested more in her parents' thriving acreage than Maria. But, the now-clearly pregnant young girl's heart belonged to Sam, who, unbeknownst to her, was facing his own heartache.

Sam and his partner arrived at the shipwrecks too late. Spain had already hired divers who had gathered what they could. In Florida, Sam heard of the bold move of one Capt. Henry James, an English privateer who raided the Spanish fort where the salvaged treasure was stored. Sam called for a meeting of his crew. They had two options: go home broke or, like Captain James, "go on the account"—turn pirate. The vote was unanimous in favor of becoming indiscriminate looters of nations. As the black flag with skull and crossbones was hoisted, Sam was said to have declared: "Never again will you be slaves of the wealthy. From this day we are new men. Free men."

Back on the Cape, Maria gave birth to a baby boy bearing the telltale marks of his father: jet black hair and eyes as dark as coal. She hid the baby in the nearby barn of Elder John Knowles and crept out each night to feed the baby boy. Less than a week into his short life, the baby died. Whether it was from exposure to the cold and dampness or, as one dramatic rendering has it, from choking on a piece of straw, the tragedy did not end there. Farmer Knowles found the baby and laid in wait for the return of the child's mother. When the unsuspecting Maria returned to care for her child, Knowles accused her of infanticide. The town's selectmen ordered her confined to an Eastham prison to await trial. Maria proved as "wild as the Nauset wind;" no sooner had the iron key clicked in the lock than Maria wriggled free.

Her recapture proved to be an easy task. The sheriff would check the apple orchard, and if he didn't find her sitting there, knees clasped to her chest, then he would go a short distance further and apprehend the slight figure on the dunes silhouetted against the sea. Rumors started to fly about her escapades. Maria was either casting a spell on her jailers, bewitching them to gain her freedom,

High on the cliffs of Wellfleet, Maria kept watch for Sam's sails.

or she had signed a pact with the devil, selling her soul in exchange for the promise of being reunited with her beloved.

The sheriff tired of the chase. The case never went to trial, and the town's people wanted her gone from their community. She was stoned away from Eastham as a witch. Such was the paranoia of the time. Unlike Salem, the Cape did not hang its witches. Stoning or a whipping at the stocks provided sufficient punishment. Maria had no illusions that she would ever be able to live among her family, relatives, or friends again. She retreated to an abandoned hut near the shoreline of what is now Marconi Beach in Wellfleet. High on the cliffs she could keep watch to the east for the first sign of Sam's sails. It would be a long wait.

Following their disappointment in Florida, Bellamy and Williams teamed up with pirate captain Henry Jennings. The band of pirates headed to Cuba and encountered the *Ste. Marie,* a French merchant ship with a cargo of twenty-eight thousand Spanish pieces of eight. Bellamy double-crossed Jennings and, in a daring raid, captured the heavily armed *Ste. Marie.* From Cuba, Bellamy, along with Williams, set up a base of operations off the coast of Belize in Central America. There they picked up a New England Native American tribal member, John Julian, as their newest pirate cohort and guide. They then joined forces with Benjamin Hornigold, a master of the pirate arts. Hornigold took a liking to the young upstart and gave Bellamy the *Marianne,* a New England-built, single-decked sloop capable of carrying forty tons of booty. The *Marianne* was Bellamy's first real pirate ship.

On the high seas in June of 1716, the flotilla of pirates surrounded a ship flying the English flag. Some pirates have scruples. Hornigold, an Englishman, decreed that his fellow pirates could confiscate the liquor on board but not the cargo. Bellamy and Hornigold argued. The crew took a vote. Hornigold was outvoted in favor of Bellamy's leadership. Capt. Black Bellamy began ruling the seas. Over the course of the next twelve months, Bellamy and his crew took booty from fifty-two ships from an array of nations. In September 1716, the captured ship *Sultana* became Bellamy's new flagship. Williams, his steadfast partner, captained the *Marianne.*

In February of 1717, after giving chase for three days, they captured their biggest prize yet—the *Whydah,* a three-hundred-ton galley. Captained by Lawrence Prince, the *Whydah* engaged in the lucrative slave trade. Capt. Prince had just sold his illicit cargo of six hundred slaves and was on the homeward leg of his journey. When Bellamy boarded the *Whydah,* he found hundreds of elephant tusks, bags of lapis-blue dye, sacks of sugar, and casks of molasses. Deep in the hold, the stunned crew uncovered sacks of silver and gold, African Akan gold jewelry, and, according to rumor, a small casket of East Indian jewels with a ruby the size of a hen's egg. It was by far the biggest single haul made by pirates in the Caribbean in decades.

As Sam's fortunes rose, his erstwhile lover's plummeted. Ostracized and alone, she often dreamed that her Sam was walking across the waters to fetch her. Her hallucinations conjured up images of a flotilla of ghost ships slipping through the fog, with Sam at the helm of the flagship. In her nightmares, a slick, well-dressed man brandishing a gold-tipped cane stood over her—the devil exacting his due.

Maria survived on fish and fowl from the nearby ponds and forest. In exchange for bread and supplies, she took in weaving. Although people continued to think her a witch who danced on Sabbath nights in the hollow by the Burying Acre, a witch who had signed a pact with the devil for Sam's soul, no woman on the peninsula could weave patterns as intricate as Goody Hallett. (Goody was a term of address akin to Mrs., and the women of Eastham were more comfortable limiting their interactions to strictly formal ones.) Casual small talk did not enter into the conversation when trading with the witch. Since there was no chit-chat or gossip, Goody Hallett remained ignorant about her lover's unlawful actions.

In the spring of 1717, the *Whydah* groaned as her bow turned to the north. After eighteen months at sea, it was time to divide the spoils, repair the boats, and plan for the future. The *Whydah's* hull, as along with that of the *Marianne,* was filled to capacity with precious treasure from around the globe. But even as they headed for the colonies, perhaps with Cape Cod as a final destination, Bellamy ordered his crew to continue to plunder. Without warning, winds from a frigid nor'easter collided with a warm and moist southern wind. The greatest storm to hit the Cape, fueled by winds as high as eighty miles per hour, seas cresting at forty to fifty feet, and zero visibility, rendered navigation useless. First, the *Marianne* grounded on the shoals, and then the *Whydah* hit a sandbar five hundred yards from shore. Buried by tons of water, the *Whydah* rolled over. Sailors were swept out to sea or crushed to death under the weight of falling cannons and sacks of gold.

To Goody Hallett, it was just another shipwreck among the thousands that occurred along the graveyard coastline of the lower Cape. She, like the other town folk, stepped over bodies that washed ashore, seeking to salvage whatever goods might be among the debris. It was only after she turned to take her meager findings back to her hut that she overhead the names of the doomed ship and its pirate captain, Black Sam Bellamy. Even if she thought one of the battered corpses might have been Sam, she would have found it nearly impossible to recognize his features after the relentless sea and pounding surf disfigured and maimed the bodies.

Tallies vary slightly as to the number of dead and missing. Over the course of several days of diving and excavation, *Whydah* salvager Barry Clifford analyzed that there were 146 men on board: 130 pirates and 16 prisoners. Only 2 were known to have survived. Neither of these was Bellamy. Washed up on the beach were 102 bodies, leaving 44 unaccounted for.

This haunted tale survives at the crossroads of fact and fantasy, the junction of legend and lore. Some say that for the rest of her days, Maria Hallett returned to the beach, but never found Sam or peace. She went mad; her wails and screeches were heard for miles. Maria's body was found on the beach. She committed suicide by slitting her throat, but her terrible anguish did not die with her. Maria's ghost walks the cliffs of Wellfleet and begs for answers.

Like all good folklore, there's always a twist. In another version, after Sam went down with his ship, his enduring love for the enchanting Eastham girl lived on. His ghost returns to reunite with the ever-faithful spirit of Maria. To those who claim to witness the apparitions on Marconi beach, the courtship flourishes. Sam's spirit rides the crest of a wave rolling into shore. He seeks the fragile shape of his love and comforts her. Together, the phantom couple stroll the beach, two ghostly forms melding into one.

Some oral history accounts say that a few weeks after the wreck, a dark-haired stranger showed up at the tavern. He had a deep scar across his forehead. When he spoke, his words were muddled and confused. He seemed to be seeking something or someone. The disheveled stranger was tolerated at the tavern because of his ability to pay for his ale. Like a magician pulling a rabbit out of his hat, the peculiar man would pluck silver or a gold coin from a dirty girdle bound tightly to his waist. Then, the stranger abruptly disappeared.

Rumors flew—the stranger must have been Black Sam Bellamy. He had survived—so strong was his love for Maria that even stunned by a blow to the head and tossed roughly ashore, his mind clung to only the thought of finding the girl he left behind. More rumors circulated. A proper Puritan matron repeated to all who would listen that as she had approached Goody Hallett's hut in the days prior to her suicide, she heard a male and female voice arguing. Offended by the vile language, she did not enter the hut to deliver wool for Goody to weave nor ascertain who was inside. She turned away and hastened to her home in Eastham.

There were dark undertones and malevolent forces at work. Maria had delivered a child alone, and mourned its death. She had been arrested, accused of fornication and infanticide, jailed and stoned out of town as a witch and a whore—all before reaching her sixteenth birthday. The gossip mongers claimed her pact with the devil was not for Sam's safe return but rather for revenge on the man who had abandoned her. Like the legendary sea witch of Billingsgate who created havoc for sailors on the high seas, Maria joined in cursing every man, especially Sam, who so cavalierly left their womenfolk behind. In exchange for her soul, Maria asked the devil for power to control the sea. Indeed, the *Whydah* went down in the fiercest nor'easter ever to hit the Cape.

"I have no doubt that Goody had a hand in brewing the April hurricane that brought on disaster to Bellamy's ship, the *Whidah*," declared Jeremiah Digges. Digges was the pen name for Joseph Berger, who wrote about Goody Hallet in *Cape Cod Pilot,* a 1937 compilation of the Federal Writers Project.

After salvaging whatever treasure she could from what was

scattered on the beach, Maria befriended one of the survivors, Indian John. In exchange for hiding him from the authorities, the Indian confided in Maria that in the hours before the wreck, each man on board had stuffed his pockets and girdled a cloth around his waist with as much gold and silver coins as they could grab. He knew where the other survivors have hidden their secret cache.

The mysterious stranger might not have been as befuddled as he appeared. He sought news of any recovered treasure from the *Whydah*. On learning that Maria was living in a hut and that a man with the features of an Indian might be hiding nearby, the stranger confronted Maria. Both had aged considerably. Maria's once silken hair was matted and dirty, her blue eyes sunken and hollow. This is not the delicate, fair-skinned beauty of whom he dreamt during so many long nights at sea. The woman before him had wrinkles and blemishes, skin spotted like worn brown leather. This was a foul-smelling, angry creature whose features contorted at the sight of *him*, a sallow, sickly man, not the dashing figure of her innocent youth. Gouges and scars marred his face, arms, and hands. His teeth were rotting and yellow. Gray streaks cut through dull black hair.

The meeting ended in a shouting match. He demanded the return of his treasure. She screamed that he will never see one more coin in his lifetime. He drew a short, sharp-edged knife. She produced an equally vicious blade hidden in her ample bodice. Both suffered fatal wounds. In the dim pre-dawn light, a lone fisherman, walking the beach below the cliffs, stumbled over two bodies.

On Marconi Beach in Wellfleet, two angry wraiths are locked in battle. On stormy nights, the pounding waves toss this phantom pair on to the beach. They emerge from the dingy foam tangled together, almost indistinguishable from the other flotsam and jetsam if not for the screeches and screams that envelop them.

One haunted tale of a pirate and his would-be bride provides a choice of various endings: the wailing ghost of Maria, mad and alone; the reunited spirits of lovers Sam and Maria; and the angry wraiths—the pirate and the witch—at each other's throats.

A mysterious necklace of gold beads, kept by a Mary Hallett.

Lagniappe: Barry Clifford, who discovered the wreck of the pirate ship *Whydah,* Ken Kinkor, late historian at the Whydah Museum in Provincetown, and a host of other researchers, folklorists, and writers all agree that Black Sam Bellamy was the most daring and successful pirate of the eighteenth century. The love story of Sam and Maria, while passed down from generation to generation for nearly three hundred years, is a bit harder to authenticate. Maria Hallett is the true unknown in this equation. Her starring role defies attempts to document her existence. She is most often referred to as Maria Hallett, and later, after her stoning in Eastham and her escape to her Wellfleet hut, as Goody Hallett. As pointed out by Clifford, Kinkor, and biographer Kathleen Brunelle, Maria was an unusual name for Puritan New England, as it was more often associated with families of a predominately Catholic region. The Halletts of Cape Cod had no daughters by the name of Maria. Mary, Mercy, Mehitable are among those listed in Hallett genealogy records. During his exhaustive research, historian Kinkor uncovered an important document related to one Mary Hallet, born 1693 and never married.

In her will, dated April 1751, Mary Hallet divided all her worldly possessions among her surviving sisters, brothers, nieces, and nephews, with one remarkable exception—a string of price-less gold beads. The will reads in part: "I give and bequeath to my sister, Hope Griffith, my wearing appearell, including two gold rings but not my gold beads." This Mary Hallett is very attached to her prized piece of jewelry, and it seem that she took the necklace with her to the grave. It is unlikely that a proper unmarried woman of this era would have received such an unusual and expensive necklace as a gift. The beads were not passed down from her family, as there is no record of them in her parents' estate. Were these golden beads part of the *Whydah* treasure?

If Mary Hallett of Yarmouth was the Maria Hallett of legend, then the ghostly pair who haunts Marconi Beach could not be the eternally wrathful spirits but rather the loving couple, reunited. Barry Clifford would prefer to think that the tale of the two lovers is true. "It's one of the things that caught my attention as a young person . . . it's a Cape folk story that I've always liked to believe."

The Whydah *and its pirate treasure wrecked in a storm off of Cape Cod.* (Photograph by Russell Sillery)

12

The Ghosts of the
Whydah Expedition

*I have learned to expect the unexpected, but I still find it hard to deal with
the unexplained. Things that go bump in the night are bothersome to me, not
because they are frightening, but because I don't know how they happen or why.*

—Barry Clifford, *Expedition Whydah*

For most New Englanders, Thanksgiving is celebrated as a time to
reflect and be grateful. For salvager Barry Clifford, Thanksgiving
1981 was the start of a grueling quest. Dinner that year was at
the home of Pulitzer Prize-winning author William Styron. Over
after-dinner drinks, Clifford shared the tantalizing tale of the
wreck of the pirate ship *Whydah.* As his passion for the story of
Capt. Black Sam Bellamy unfolded, a fellow guest, a legendary
CBS news anchor, was intrigued: "It was Walter Cronkite, and he
asked me what I was doing about it. I told him I was thinking about
going to look for a shipwreck on the Cape called the *Whydah.*"
Cronkite threw down the gauntlet. "Why don't you do it?"

After an unrelenting saga on land and sea, Barry Clifford did
just that. The *Whydah,* a former slave ship captured by pirate Sam
Bellamy, is the only authenticated pirate shipwreck ever found,
and her treasures are still being recovered—with a few nudges
from the spirit world.

In April 1983, Clifford set up his land-based operations at
the Captain Heman Smith House, a two-story colonial near
Jeremiah's Gutter in Orleans. Jeremiah's Gutter was the first
canal to cut across the Cape peninsula, connecting Cape Cod Bay

to the Atlantic Ocean. Prior to his salvage crew's arrival, Clifford had a haunting dream: Emerging from the muck of Jeremiah's Gutter was a parade of ragged men. If the proximity to the Gutter crept into Clifford's subconscious it produced some intimidating imagery of men dressed like pirates and covered with seaweed and sand. The menacing phantoms strode across the lawn of the Captain house, barged through the front door, stomped single file up the stairs to Clifford's room, and shoved the door open. Jarred from sleep, Clifford flipped on the light fully expecting to see ". . . a room full of pirates protesting the fact that I was searching for their booty," but the room was devoid of phantoms. The

The Whydah Museum houses the artifacts brought up from the wreck.

bedroom door remained securely closed. There were no telltale muddy footprints or slimy strands of seaweed. Nothing to indicate that the pirate ghosts existed ". . . anywhere but in my head."

Still, the images lingered. Deciphering the meaning of any dream or nightmare is always a toss-up. Either the grim ghosts were hostile and didn't want Clifford to search for the booty they had worked so hard for, or the spirited pirates from the past were welcoming him to their watery lair. At the time, Clifford elected to take a positive view, believing that this was an invitation to search for the *Whydah*. Looking back on the decades-old dream of phantom pirates tracking him down, the successful discoverer of the wreck of the *Whydah* shrugs it off. "I guess I was just thinking about them."

Today, sitting in his private quarters on the second floor over the Whydah Museum on MacMillan Wharf in Provincetown, Barry Clifford is a striking presence. A shaved head emphasizes piercing sea-blue eyes. A black tee-shirt shows off a diver's well-toned physique molded by thirty-plus years on the open water. His ship, the *Vast Explorer,* a gleaming white sixty-five-foot vessel, is tied to the dock below. Clifford is impatient. Now that he has found the *Whydah*, his focus is on the on-going excavation. The 2013 season could promise a peek at the mother lode of Bellamy's treasure. Barry Clifford is guarded about what is next on the agenda.

Seeking a pirate shipwreck and her scattered treasure lost for more than 250 years in the ever-shifting sands of an undersea world is a daunting undertaking. Wading through a sea of ancient court documents, records, and obscure maps to pinpoint the location is equally frustrating. In the early stages of the research process, Clifford became a man obsessed. Skeptics saw him as a dreamer, out of touch with reality. Clifford readily admits he had his moments. In his book about the expedition, several inexplicable incidents are revealed.

In attempting to recall the events, Clifford said he had a lot on his mind at the time. His thoughts had drifted to the Capt. Cyprian Southack, the eighteenth-century captain appointed by

A scale model of Black Sam Bellamy's ship is on display in the museum.

the British governor to recover treasure from the wreck of the *Whydah*. Southack recovered bodies from the beach, but failed to retrieve any treasure. While driving around one morning, Clifford pulled up to a stoplight, and an image of the scowling face of Captain Southhack materialized inches from his own. The phantom figure seemed to be holding a map in his hand as he scanned the land for familiar landmarks. A honking of a car horn behind him interrupted Clifford's reverie, and the ghostly searcher dissipated.

While a chance to have a conversation with Capt. Southack eluded him, another ghost hung around long enough to offer a few valuable clues. Again expressing reluctance to dwell on ghostly images, Clifford remembers a second vivid dream. He and Black Sam Bellamy were standing on the deck of a ship. Beneath them, the ocean had an eerie stillness, a dead calm. Abruptly, a soundtrack kicked in: laughter punctuated by high-decibel screams from a cacophony of disembodied voices was immediately followed by a dialogue between the twenty-first-century explorer and the 1717 ghost captain. Initially, the spirit of Black Sam responded with only a disdainful leer when asked if they were closing in on the wreck of the *Whydah*. The imposing phantom nodded in the affirmative, and then spoke in a brusque voice: "You are close, but too close to shore." This was followed by another hint that things are "not what they used to be." The combination of these clues, although veiled and vague, propelled Clifford awake. Despite the three a.m. predawn hour, he called Stretch Grey, his trusted captain, and shouted into the phone, "I know where the *Whydah* is!" Grey hung up on him. Clifford redialed. In a rush of words he blurted that the wreck was farther out. In his dream, Sam Bellamy ". . . told me where to look."

Clifford relates that when the rest of the crew heard about his alleged conversation with the long-dead pirate, they thought he had finally gone insane. They insisted the search continue where they were presently anchored near shore. The first season of searching for the *Whydah* ended in defeat. Unfazed, Clifford remained steadfast in his conviction that psycho-imaging, which he defines as using ". . . paranormal methods to find artifacts instead of the magnetometer," would be an asset in their quest during a resumed search the following year.

On July 20, 1984, during the second season, an NBC camera crew was on board the *Vast Explorer*. The sky was nearly clear—only one small cloud hovered on the horizon. The plan was to get footage as the divers searched a new site. Having come up empty-handed at fifty other sites, the mood topside bordered on hopelessness. A diver went down. He reappeared in a flash, as if he had seen a shark or the looming ghost of Sam Bellamy.

His discovery was better than a phantom pirate—the diver had spotted three cannons. A second diver pulled up a cannon ball encrusted with a gold coin, a Spanish piece of eight with markings dating it to 1688. With proof that the *Whydah* was below them, the mood turned jubilant. Overhead, the small dark cloud moved stealthily to a position directly over the boat. There was a bright flash of lighting and deafening clap of thunder. One startled crew member proclaimed, "It's Sam Bellamy!" Captain Grey added a terse observation that the pirates didn't want to be found.

Clifford remembers the odd weather phenomenon. "Just right after we found the shipwreck, you know, a thunderstorm came over the top of the ship . . . it was a turning point for us, the thunderstorm. I guess you could extrapolate that into anything,

Strange things continued to happen on Vast Explorer, *Clifford's research vessel.*

A pewter plate and spoon were among the everyday artifacts recovered from the debris field.

but it just happened at the time we found the wreck. Yeah, I would say a strange coincidence."

After the mini-storm passed, the divers recovered a glittering hoard of gold and silver coins. In one twenty-minute period, Clifford alone brought up 280 coins. Clifford says that he wanted to hold them close, not for their value, but for the secrets they surely held. These were the very reason the men had turned pirates.

Everyday items—pewter plates, forks, spoons, a tankard—underscored the human connection. One item—a leather shoe with the leg bone still attached—sent shock waves through the crew. Protected from decay by concretion from a cannon that had pinned the doomed sailor to the sea floor, the size-five men's shoe with its silk stocking was of a style worn by someone from the upper class, not your average pirate. "It was years later that we were able to decipher that," states Clifford.

After the discovery of the shoe and leg bone, the *Whydah* research director, the late Ken Kinkor, began poring over primary source documents. In a 1716 Antigua court deposition, Capt. Abijah Savage testified that his passenger ship, the *Bonetta,* was overtaken by the pirate ship *Marianne,* then captained by Sam Bellamy. For fifteen days, the pirates plundered and intimidated the passengers, taking away anything of value. Two of the *Bonetta*'s crew switched allegiance and joined the pirates. One small boy watched in wonder, then announced he was going, too. Young John King was traveling with his mother from Antigua to Jamaica. John's mother refused her son's request. However, the willful child prevailed. According to Captain Savage, the boy was neither forced nor coerced. "He declared he would Kill himself if he was Restrained, and even threatened his Mother who was then on Board as a passenger with Deponent."

Clifford shakes his head in genuine puzzlement. "I was wondering why he would threaten his mother and join the pirate crews—and what kind of a mother she was. The question is: What was going on aboard the pirate ship that looked so exciting for him? So, he must have seen things going on on the pirate ship that attracted him if the primary source documents are correct." When Sam Bellamy replaced the *Marianne* with the *Whydah* as his flag ship, the littlest pirate, John King, went along.

The shoe and leg bone sat in storage until Kinkor had the bone examined by the Center for Historical Archaeology and the Smithsonian Institution. The examinations confirmed the bone to be that of a child between the ages of eight and eleven. To date, no other historical records have revealed that a child so young was allowed to sign up with a nefarious band of buccaneers. In trying to picture what it was like the day little John King sealed his fate, Kinkor speculated that Bellamy must have admired his spirit.

Black Sam Bellamy proudly flew the Jolly Roger on the Whydah.

"I could almost see him begging Bellamy to let him join, and Bellamy not having the heart to refuse him." A human artifact, like this child's shoe, serves as a chilling reminder of the perils of a pirate's life.

While a total of 12,107 artifacts were brought to the surface during the second season, doubters remained. The artifacts proved that this was the wreck of an eighteenth-century ship, but not necessarily the *Whydah*. Shifting sands or devious phantom pirates at work had hidden the physical evidence needed in a pit forty-five feet deep. The *Whydah*'s cast bronze bell, indisputable proof that this wreck was indeed the tomb of pirates who sailed with Black Sam Bellamy, did not come to the surface until the summer of 1985. With it came a surprise. Until the encrustations fell away, the spelling of the name of Bellamy's ship had been recorded in documents as "Whidah." Nearly three centuries later, the error would be corrected. The name, *THE WHYDAH GALLY 1716,* was emblazoned around the upper band of the bell. The headline on the November 1, 1985, edition of the *New York Times* proclaimed, "Bell Confirms That Salvors Found Pirate Ship of Legend." The bell, as reported in the article, declared that this was "The first identification in history of a pirate ship." Still, the troublesome ghosts did not fade quietly into the night, nor did the operation proceed on an even keel.

The salvage operation continued, but the number of recovered artifacts dwindled. Expenses mounted: preservation costs, administrative overhead, equipment maintenance and repairs. Clifford argued valiantly that they had not yet hit the mother lode. The investors grumbled, lost faith, and pulled the plug. Despite all the success and notoriety, the site was closed. The doomed souls of the *Whydah* could return to their watery grave and be hassle free.

Still, Barry Clifford could not let go. In 1998, almost fourteen years after locating the bell, this underwater explorer and avid preservationist resumed operations—and the aggravated pirates appeared to fire a few warning shots across his bow. On the first attempt out to the site, an engine malfunction triggered an on-board scramble to make repairs. With the engine finally running, a thick fog rolled in, limiting visibility to less than one hundred yards. Glitches in the new GPS blocked the crew from plotting coordinates of the artifacts on the site map. Resigned to their fate that this trip was a no-go, they made a U-turn back to the dock—with near-disastrous results. In the impenetrable fog, they relied on the GPS, which misdirected them straight into the shallow waters of the shore. The hull of the research vessel hit bottom. Clifford assessed their narrow escape from disaster. Without fast reaction time, powerful engines allowing them to reverse course, and a large helping of luck, they would have ended up on the same beach as Bellamy and his crew. It appeared as if the doomed pirates were toying with the crew of the *Vast,* giving them a glimpse of what they had faced in those final fatal moments—a cruel taunt from beyond the grave.

Clifford's passion to be on "the trail of something big" was palpable. He was convinced they would find the *Whydah* when "the pirates thought we had earned it." Recalling the details of the averted catastrophe with the flawed GPS, Clifford points out that, "It was thirty years ago. It happens a lot . . . a couple of years ago our rudder broke and we turned around and headed into shore. There's been a bunch of incidents like that."

A new member of the team, Chris Macort, was convinced that the pirates were trying to establish communications. Macort had been aboard the *Crumpstey,* their back-up vessel, when the radio began to crackle. Cutting through the static was a voice. He cranked up the volume to hear demands: "We want your boat. We want your boat." On the next visit to the site, Macort brought along a bottle of rum, announcing that he had figured out what the pirates craved, and poured the contents of the bottle into the ocean swells.

A broad smile lights up the face of expedition leader Clifford as he recalls the ritual. "That was just one of those fun things that you do. Chris poured some rum into the water just to, you know, appease the pirates." The offering was well received. That season was one of the best ever. Divers sucked up a river of gold dust with a turkey baster and brought to the surface a grinding stone and a rare swivel cannon.

Strange things continued to happen. In July 1998, Clifford and crew were accompanied by photographers and a writer from the *National Geographic*. Unfortunately, visibility below was poor, and the underwater photographers were frustrated. There would be one last try in the morning. That night, the pirates paid another spirited call. Those sleeping below decks awoke at two a. m. to a terrifying crash and piercing scream, as if someone had fallen or was pushed overboard. A head count showed that all eleven people on the *Vast Explorer* were accounted for. The next thought was that another boat had collided with the *Crumpstey,* the whaler tied behind the *Vast.* A flashlight inspection showed all was well. Another bloodcurdling scream split the air. Crewmate Macort was convinced this time that it wasn't the intimidation factor of the pirates of the *Whydah* but rather Captain Crumpstey's irate ghost. Crumpstey had been captain of the *Marianne,* a ship laden with seven thousand gallons of Maderia wine that the pirates of the *Whydah* had confiscated for their own pleasure. To placate the enraged captain, Macort repeated his new-found alcoholic ritual. He poured a bottle of wine over the waters, and the screaming stopped.

In the morning, it was Macort's turn to dive. At thirty-two feet, the youthful diver found a long, curving section of the *Whydah*'s hull. A portion of the bulkhead was lined with metal. It was the gunpowder room near what would have been Sam Bellamy's quarters. When Clifford dove down to inspect the astonishing find, his thoughts gravitated inevitably to the men, the most successful pirates of their time, who went down with the ship: "This was their tomb."

Through years of agonizing trial and error, success and disappointments, a roller coaster of emotions, a philosophical Clifford summed up his feelings in *Expedition Whydah:* "I was not insane or irrational for believing that the spirits of the dead buccaneers looked over the wreck of their ship . . . taking another man's booty isn't supposed to be easy . . . eventually you have to contend with the real owners."

Lagniappe: Housed in a colonial-era home on Main Street in Wellfleet, Aesop's Tables was a popular Cape Cod restaurant. Centuries earlier, Sam Bellamy may well have passed this spot as he strolled through town. In 1998, Barry Clifford, some of his crew, and the crew from the National Geographic had just finished dinner the night before they went out on the *Vast Explorer* and subsequently discovered the hull of the *Whydah*. After they left, an incident occurred that raises many eyebrows. A man, eating dinner alone at the far end of the bar, went to the restroom. He came out white and shaking. He announced that he had to leave the restaurant immediately. His server asked what was wrong. "You might think I am going crazy here, but I just saw a ghost in your bathroom." The frightened man said the ghost was a young woman with pale blond hair and an ability to make the room frigid in July. His description of the female apparition matched the profile often attributed to Maria Hallett, Black Sam Bellamy's lover. The agitated patron signed the credit card slip and made a quick exit. The waitress repeated what he said to her manager. The manager followed up. He went into the bathroom to check it out, and found nothing. He asked the waitress for the name of her customer. She flipped through her receipts. "Here it is—the name is Bellamy." Aesop's Tables closed in 2004. The historic former captain's house has reopened as Winslow's Tavern. There have been no recent reports of a lovely female ghost startling guests in the bathroom.

The Whydah Museum in Provincetown preserves and houses the artifacts salvaged from the *Whydah*. For all those who have ever harbored a secret yearning to uncover their own sunken treasure, this museum will transport you into Sam Bellamy's world and allow you to view the treasures hidden for almost three centuries in the sea bottom off Cape Cod. However, Clifford is adamant about not applying the term "treasure hunter" to his work.

"Treasure hunters sell treasure. We've never sold any treasure. The project is about archeology—digging up the ships, preserving the ships for posterity and for historical reasons." As for the ghosts of the *Whydah,* he is less rigid: "For fun, I'll talk about a ghost thing, but it's not something I spend a lot of time thinking about."

Update February 12, 2021: "Six Skeletons Found in Wreck of 18th-Century Pirate Ship Sunk Off Cape Cod." The prestigious *Smithsonian Magazine* reported on a shocking new discovery from the wreck of the *Whydah.* The article revealed that a team led by Barry Clifford, who discovered the wreck in 1984 and continues to dive at the site, found the skeletal remains of six crew members inside huge concretions (masses that form around underwater objects). It was determined that some bones in the remains were likely broken when the ship capsized, crushing the men. In a statement quoted by CBS News, Clifford said, "We hope that modern, cutting-edge technology will help us identify these pirates and reunite them with any descendants who could be out there." Barry Clifford remains optimistic that one day, continued research will lead them to the remains of the *Whydah*'s legendary captain, Black Sam Bellamy.

The Whydah Museum in Provincetown has closed, but the new expanded Whydah Pirate Museum in Yarmouth showcases even more pirate treasure, with exhibits that the ghosts of Sam and his pirate crew would surely be happy to haunt.

Epilogue

Not all who wander are lost.
—J. R. R. Tolkien, *The Fellowship of the Ring*

Will there ever be a day when we'll know with absolute certainty that spirits of the dead can slip back and forth between our world and theirs? We are left to rely on our own experiences and those of family, friends, and passing acquaintances. We choose to accept or reject the validity of many an oft-told tale.

The love story of Maria Hallett and Sam Bellamy is one of the most enduring legends on Cape Cod. The Sandwich Glass Museum created holograms of Rebecca and William Burgess, giving visitors the illusion that this couple still yearn and grieve for each other. Bill Putman has only one ghost to look after, and he is satisfied that little Susan is happy at the Simmons Homestead.

Whether they are born from a need to believe that death is not the end, that some form of life endures, haunted tales make the implausible seem plausible. They impart a sense of hope, a connection to the past—and that will do for now.

I am grateful to the many generous residents of Cape Cod who shared their stories with me: Derek Bartlett, Barry Clifford, Shelly Conway, Ken Kinkor, Marianne McCaffery, Malcom Perna, George A. Phelps, Bill Putman, Ed Sabin, Shirley Sabin, and everyone who added their own special twist to the tales.

Additional thanks to the National Park Service for the photo of Edward Penniman, and the Falmouth Historical Society and archivist Meg Costello for research materials and photos. Thank

A lighthouse on the Upper Cape, guiding sailors home.

you to the librarians and staff at the Masphee Public Library for your invaluable assistance.

A special thank-you to friends and family for their continued support: my brother, Russell Sillery, for his haunting images of Maria and Sam and the pirate ship; my son-in-law, Tim Moore; my daughters, Danielle Genter Moore, Rebecca Genter, and Heather Genter. To Michael Moore and Leila Sillery Moore for proving that ghost stories appeal to all ages. And to my friend Patricia Dottore, who accompanied me on some of these amazing adventures, which resulted in many new and surprising chapters. May the sea gods be with you all.

Appendix

For more information about the historic sites in this book, or to take a personal tour, the following is a list of their locations on Cape Cod.

Captain Bangs Hallet House Museum
11 Strawberry Lane, Yarmouth Port

Captain Linnell House
137 Skaket Beach Road, Orleans

Chapter House (former Colonial House Inn)
277 Route 6A, Yarmouth Port

Edward Gorey House
8 Strawberry Lane, Yarmouth Port

Museums on the Green
Dr. Wicks/Captain Bourne House
55-65 Palmer Avenue, Falmouth

Penniman House
Fort Hill Road, Eastham

Provincetown Library
356 Commercial Street, Provincetown

Sandwich Glass Museum
129 Main Street, Sandwich

Simmons Homestead Inn
288 Scudder Avenue, Hyannis Port

Whydah Pirate Museum
674 Route 28, Yarmouth

(Author photo courtesy of Jeffery D. Meyers)